On December 7, 2011, I r[...]
General Reno on the Sena[...]
leader, superb officer, and friend." I did not exaggerate. I personally worked with him during my years in the Senate. The author of *10 Leadership Maneuvers* is a humble man of God who has served and led with great distinction. I salute him and urge you to read this excellent book.

JAMES INHOFE, SENIOR US SENATOR FROM OKLAHOMA

This book will inspire you. It has me. I have known Lieutenant General (Ret.) Reno and benefitted from his wise counsel and wonderful leadership. I think you will too.

MARY FALLIN, 27TH GOVERNOR OF OKLAHOMA
FORMER US REPRESENTATIVE

Loren Reno is my friend. He and I began our work together when we were lieutenants and rejoined later in our careers when he was a lieutenant general. Throughout his notable tenure in our Air Force, he was a consistent and compelling leader of small and large organizations alike. I truly admire all he stands for and the leadership qualities he writes of and lives.

NORTON A. SCHWARTZ, GENERAL, USAF (RET)
19TH USAF CHIEF OF STAFF

I first encountered Loren Reno when I worked his first Colonel assignment in the Air Force. Our friendship now spans more than two decades, and I am blessed by it. His prescriptions for effective living and leadership are what I see in his life. I was honored to make comment on his early drafts and humbled to provide some illustrations. A life well lived; a book well written.

I'm grateful he shared them both with me, and now with his readers.

ROGER A. BRADY, GENERAL, USAF (RET), AUTHOR OF *FORGET SUCCESS!!* AND *NOTHING HAS CHANGED: A YEAR OF DAILY DEVOTIONALS*.

I give Lt. Gen. (Ret.) Reno my complete endorsement—to his book and to him. He is a true man of God and the leadership experience he has brought to Cedarville University has made the institution and its leaders stronger. Seeing "serving" as a thread running through this book is no surprise if you know the author. You'll want to read this cover-to-cover, and then come study with a giant example of great leadership in southwest Ohio. You won't regret it.

DR. THOMAS WHITE, PRESIDENT AND PROFESSOR OF THEOLOGY
CEDARVILLE UNIVERSITY

The leadership vacuum continues. Finding, developing, and training leaders is the exquisite task. Enter Lieutenant General (Ret.) Loren Reno. General Reno is a sterling example of a leader, built on a framework of integrity. His love for God's word and the military come together to explain leadership. Not only is he my friend, he has encouraged me to be a better leader. He lives what he writes and you are handling a great book.

DR. MICHAEL EASLEY, TEACHING PASTOR
FELLOWSHIP BIBLE CHURCH, BRENTWOOD TN
AUTHOR, RADIO HOST OF MICHAEL EASLEY INCONTEXT
FORMER PRESIDENT AND CEO, MOODY BIBLE INSTITUTE

Loren Reno is a proven leader. When he and his family attended the church I pastor, Loren served our nation at the highest levels of military service and yet worked every Sunday in our church nursery. He's a leader who serves. These leadership maneuvers have been forged in the crucible of experience and time in God's

Word. I'm thankful he is sharing what he's learned with us. When a man like Loren speaks about leadership I want to listen, and you should too. I highly recommend *10 Leadership Maneuvers*.

DR. MARK HITCHCOCK, IS SENIOR PASTOR, FAITH BIBLE CHURCH (EDMOND, OK); ASSOCIATE PROFESSOR OF BIBLE EXPOSITION, DALLAS THEOLOGICAL SEMINARY; AUTHOR OF OVER 20 BOOKS INCLUDING: *IRAN AND ISRAEL: WARS AND RUMORS OF WARS; THE END: A COMPLETE OVERVIEW OF BIBLE PROPHECY AND THE END OF DAYS; AND CASHLESS: BIBLE PROPHECY, ECONOMIC CHAOS, AND THE FUTURE FINANCIAL ORDER*

In uniform, Loren Reno's leadership was respected far and wide by his peers and especially by those he led. In writing, Loren has captured three key themes that I can attest he has lived and taught: 1) integrity in action, speech, and thought; 2) service as the foundation for leadership; and 3) humility in recognizing that the leader's role, as Loren exemplifies it, reflects simultaneously being a follower, leader, and child of God. The insights, principles, and stories in this book mark valuable pathways to effective and respectful leadership. The words are absolutely consistent with the Loren Reno I know, and that's a truly wonderful thing!

CHRIS MILLER, LIEUTENANT GENERAL, USAF (RET.)

When I think of what a Servant-Leader looks like, my father comes immediately to mind. Loren Reno comes right after that! What he shares in this book comes from the deep well of a soul that God has made beautiful. Loren writes authoritatively from a wealth of military experience—thirty-eight years' worth—skillfully drawing out the biblical foundations that have shaped his amazing leadership career.

DR. JON YOUNG, SENIOR PASTOR OF
DAYTON AVENUE BAPTIST CHURCH, XENIA OH

Loren Reno writes like he lives and talks. In the forty-five years I've known him, I have visited squadrons, groups, and centers under his command. I've watched changes of command and his promotions. Lt. Gen. Reno (Ret.) is always ready to offer service and help to all, including wonderful honor to war veterans of all ages. Read about powerful serving and leading from a servant-leader.

DR. CLIFFORD JOHNSON, WWII ARMY AIR CORPS FIGHTER PILOT

I want to learn leadership from one who has led others with distinction. I want to follow the person who has discovered and successfully applied timeless truths. Lieutenant General (Ret.) Loren Reno is that person. A remarkable military career has been the proving ground. *10 Leadership Maneuvers* qualifies as a life-long literary companion.

JOHN D. BECKETT, CHAIRMAN OF THE BECKETT COMPANIES
AUTHOR OF *LOVING MONDAY AND MASTERING MONDAY*

Lieutenant General (Ret.) Loren Reno is the personification of the term servant-leader. I have learned from his example and his wisdom for over thirty-five years, and I have seen firsthand the tremendous impact of the leadership principles so aptly described in his book. This is a personal and extremely practical leadership aid. Young leaders will be refreshed herein by proven insight and spurred on to excellence in serving and leading.

WILLIAM A. CHAMBERS, MAJOR GENERAL, USAF (RET.)

10 LEADERSHIP MANEUVERS

LOREN RENO

10 LEADERSHIP MANEUVERS

A GENERAL'S GUIDE TO SERVING AND LEADING

Published by
Deep River Books
Sisters, Oregon
www.deepriverbooks.com

ISBN: 9781940269542
Library of Congress: 2015937720

Printed in the USA

Cover design by Matthew Van Zomeren

To the Airmen,
with whom it has been my honor and privilege to serve.
Putting service before self, they answered their nation's call.

CONTENTS

ACKNOWLEDGMENTS

Many people have helped me to write this book. I am grateful to each one. I thank the following:

Airmen at Reserve Officer Training Corps detachments and commander's calls; several groups of captain Career Broadening Officers at the Oklahoma City Air Logistics Center; members of the Logistics Officer Association; commander designates in their pre-command orientations; and young airmen, NCOs, civilians, and officers at bases I have visited over the years for listening to me as I crafted, revised, and polished the message of this book and for their feedback and great encouragement.

Russ and Nancy Ebersole, Col. Jack Randall, Col. Bruce Mosley, MG Clay Buckingham, Maj. Gen. Don Brown, Col. Gene Ronsick, Chief Master Sergeant Kenny Dean, Col. Bill Whitaker, Lt. Gen. Trevor Hammond, Maj. Gen. Dale Tabor, Lt. Gen. Mike Zettler, Lt. Gen. Chuck Johnson, Gen. John Handy, Gen. Roger Brady, Lt. Gen. Chris Kelly, Gen. Gary "Nordo" North, Gen. Bruce Carlson, Lt. Gen. Terry Gabreski, Maj. Bill "Skipper" McClendon, Gen. Phil Breedlove, and Gen. Norton Schwartz for modeling leadership that was winsome to me and influenced me from my lieutenant to lieutenant general days.

Lee and Melanie Reno, Gordon and Candice Zimmerman, Garry and Donna Richey, Patti Ripple, Tim and Lisa Fisher, Cliff and Pam Johnson, and Don Callan for encouraging me for years to write down my stories.

Phil Schanely and Melissa Johnson at Cedarville University for helping me with the design and production of this book.

Gen. Roger Brady (USAF, Ret.) for his probing questions, insightful suggestions, and counsel, and for the illustrations in this book that are more visible than the other help he provided.

Rachel Reno, my daughter, for her relentless pursuit in correcting my grammar and offering improvements in expression. Her thirteen years of teaching students better writing habits paid off for me.

Along with Rachel, Joseph, Joshua, and Ashley, my other children, for encouraging me to "write it down."

Karen, my beloved wife, for giving up her summer plans so I could devote time to thinking and writing, for listening to the first draft of each chapter, and for reminding me of other stories to consider adding.

My Savior, Jesus Christ, for the privilege of serving and leading and for the opportunity to share some of the highlights with you.

INTRODUCTION

Let me address three questions you might have.

Why Another Book on Leadership?

There are probably thousands of books on leadership or ones that recount the biographies of leaders good and bad, recent and historic, near and far. They have been coaches, teachers, politicians, military men and women, statesmen, potentates, business executives, servants, and a Savior. Tomes tell of their speeches, writings, and actions. History tells of their successes, failures, and influence.

Add to the books all the articles in journals, the teaching in classes, and the less formal instruction along life's way for pupils, protégés, and people in general. Add to these the many seminars, courses, academic programs, and degrees that are available for people of all ages and walks of life. It's almost endless.

"Why another book on leadership?" is a fair question. Of all the leadership books I have read, I don't remember any written like this one. This book comes from my experience as a long-serving military general officer and ten things I've seen successful leaders do. It explains each of those actions, it shows their basis in Scripture, and it illustrates each with stories from my time in the U.S. Air Force.

About twenty years into my Air Force career, I began talking about leadership to young officers and civilians more than ever before. Eventually I began writing some things down, and that evolved into a PowerPoint presentation I began to use widely. Over time, I adjusted and tailored the ten actions that became the first ten chapters of this book. I had not as yet attached the biblical basis you'll find. Some of the young officers began referring to these ten actions as "Reno's Rules." I accept that characterization if by it they meant these were rules *for* me. I only offered them then (and now) for others to consider; they were not and are not "orders" in the military sense.

Many of the then-young officers, recent university students, organizational leadership groups, and others with whom I have shared these leadership actions and stories have encouraged (begged!) me to write them down. It seems that if they liked the conciseness of the actions, they really liked the stories. That's why I wrote the book.

What Do I Think Leadership Is?

There are probably as many definitions of leadership as there are books on the subject. In fact, in a class I teach on leadership at Cedarville University's school of business administration, I use a textbook that has many of these definitions. But here is how I define it:

> Leadership is the act of inspiring others to perform at a
> higher level in accomplishing a worthy goal.

I agree that leadership has many facets. While we could discuss core values, leadership attributes, worthy and unworthy examples of leaders, and so on, to do so would exceed the scope of this book. But the words I chose to use are all important. Leadership is an action. It inspires and achieves better results than giving orders. It involves others. It is performance driven, and it is often measured. It elevates. It results in an outcome, an accomplishment. It is goal driven, and the goal is worth achieving.

The overriding principle of this book is that leaders serve, as the title of Chapter 1 indicates: "The Greatest Is the Servant." In subsequent chapters, when you read about a leader, you see a servant at work. In a true leader, the servant is inseparable from the follower, the peer, and the superior.

You will see a lot of inspiration, example setting, and a focus on people. Along with serving, these are important aspects of leadership as I see it. If you think leadership is just about getting a job done without regard for others, maintaining the status quo, staying out of trouble, or avoiding risk, you will find this book uncomfortable. If, however, my definition of leadership resonates with you, you may enjoy and even benefit from it.

Why Should You Read This Book?

If you have served in the military or are attracted to the topic of military leadership at the practical level, you'll find the book most interesting. Its real stories are about real people, some of whom are worthy of emulation, while others fall short of this standard.

If you want to lead and would like advice from a seasoned practitioner, you have come to the right place. I have woven stories from my time as a new Air Force lieutenant to my retirement thirty-eight years later to illustrate what successful leaders do.

If as a parent, coach, teacher, professor, manager, administrator, or organizational officer, you want a leadership heading check, you will find application in the coming chapters.

If you are a student and wonder what leadership is all about, how you do it, and what happens when you do it right or get it wrong, read on. This pertains to high school, undergraduate, or even graduate students who see the satisfaction in leading.

If you are already in a leadership position, you will find plenty of fresh motivation here. You will see the attitudes and actions that took novice leaders to very high positions of responsibility.

If you are looking for a resource of biblical characters and references that demonstrate good leadership, you will find examples in every chapter. Each maneuver is grounded in Scripture.

If you need to think about leadership in your situation, not someone else's, Chapters 8, 9, and 10 show you a leadership model I have used and then describe how you can build one tailored to your needs. Your model will be different, but mine can show you how one looks. Chapter 11 and Appendix B show you how to construct your own.

I see this book as the tip of a leadership iceberg, an appetizer to a leadership banquet, a transition to taking your leadership to the next level. As you grow in your responsibility, I hope you find these stories from my experience a guide to developing your own leadership model. If the elapsed time since the stories occurred has eroded my recall of the accuracy of some of the details, it is entirely unintentional and my fault alone.

I place a high value on the Word of God, on serving as part of effective leadership, and on both the people part and the mission part of leading. We see a perfect illustration of this when King David, around 1000 B.C., and at the end of his life, looks back over his forty-year reign. In 2 Samuel 23:3b he says, "He that ruleth over men must be just, ruling in the fear of God." That is a good starting point for a leader and for this book. It is all about serving.

Loren Reno

ONE

THE GREATEST IS THE SERVANT

The one who serves best will lead best.

No matter the reason you might want to be a leader, or the circumstances that led to being one, or any agenda you may have inherited, the place to start is service. Being a servant is an underlying theme of this book, and it is not exhibited often in today's culture.

I define service as subordinating yourself to a larger mission with disciplined, hardscrabble self-sacrifice. Followers who aspire to be leaders deliberately put others before themselves. Sometimes leadership calls us to painful servitude; other times it means keeping our word even when it hurts. Service is neither easy nor convenient, but it does mark one for leadership.

Serving *toward* the Top

Show me a person who has been exalted, and I'll show you one who started out as a servant. This is exactly what happened with a co-pilot I knew at my first operational assignment in the Air Force in the mid-1970s.

I was a navigator in a C-130 squadron in the western Pacific. Naturally, we relied on charts and books with frequencies, approach plates, standard instrument departures, and other necessary information. The pilots and the navigator had a set of these publications for each mission. We carried all these documents in a naugahyde bag that was at least two feet long, one foot wide, and one foot deep. There might have been 100 charts, books, and supplements inside. It must have weighed fifty pounds. The bad part of this helpful and essential bag was that the contents had a shelf life; each book or chart expired at a different time. To fly with an out-of-date publication was asking for trouble. It could result in being decertified by a flight evaluator at the least, or it could result in a mishap and even loss of life at the most. It was serious business.

Keeping these documents current and ensuring that the bag had three sets of each item the crew required was a thankless job, and it wasn't always done well. Checking them all before "stepping" to the aircraft was a protracted, laborious process.

We had a co-pilot who volunteered to do this thankless job for the entire squadron. He didn't just volunteer to do it for one day; he took it on as a permanent additional duty. But like everything else he did, he did it very well. The publications were always well organized, current, and there in the right number—every flight. He came in on weekends and holidays to make sure the bags were ready for the next day's missions.

He would stay late into the night while others were relaxing at off-duty activities, just so there were no surprises for the crews.

He performed this job so well that we forgot how hard it was and how poorly it had been done before. This lieutenant co-pilot chose to be a servant. No one was surprised when, thirty years later, he became the top general in the US Air Force. He served his way toward the top.

On other occasions, I have seen a link between being a servant and being exalted. I knew another lieutenant in that first assignment who volunteered for another thankless job.

One tropical summer afternoon, a lieutenant colonel came into the squadron asking for a volunteer to sit in the unair-conditioned control tower the next day and record the times aircraft started engines, taxied, took off, landed, parked, and shut down their engines. Hoping to elude the favor seeker, people dove for cover as the uncomfortable monotony of such a task sunk in.

One lieutenant stepped forward and volunteered. He arrived early, kept precise notes not just to the minute, but to the second, for each event and sweated in the tower perch through the entire day. When the flight line was again still, he descended the long stairs and went back to the squadron where he typed (before computers) a full report with all the times, along with some other observations and explanations. He slid the report under the door of the lieutenant colonel's darkened office in another building and went home much later than most did that night.

Less than a week later, the colonel wing commander asked for that same lieutenant for an extended, special, and high-visibility job. The lieutenant colonel had recommended this specific lieutenant because of his willingness, precision, and over-and-above performance in a small matter; the wing commander knew that would be useful in larger matters. The lieutenant went on to a long and successful career in the Air Force.

He traces his successive higher positions and rank to that day in the control tower.

This lieutenant was willing to be a servant when others dove for cover, and it was an indication of his heart. The heart of the servant was even more attractive to the wise lieutenant colonel than was the report.

Serving *at* the Top

While serving is an important indicator of leadership ability for the future, it is also an indication of a leader's effectiveness in the present. I have observed that the best leaders do not stop serving after they are promoted. Continuing to serve informs the leader of needs, feedback, capacity, and high-potential individuals not always visible from the ivory tower. As the well-traveled path to the top in any organization is along the servants' trail, so the entirety of the organization is familiar territory for the effective senior leader. When leaders are done serving, they are done.

I will cover nine other leadership maneuvers in this book, and there are hundreds more that others advocate. But in my view, none is more important than remembering that the greatest leader is a servant, though this is not an original idea.

The Greatest

There are several places in the New Testament where Jesus makes clear who is the greatest. Speaking to the multitude and his disciples, Jesus said in Matthew 23:11,

But he that is greatest among you shall be your servant.

Though often interpreted to mean something different, I think it is saying clearly that Jesus is the greatest among the disciples and the multitude and that He is going to be their servant.

The act of service He was going to perform was a salvation: dying for them. He was going to serve them in this way. But He continued in the next verse talking about them:

And whosoever shall exalt himself shall be abased; and he that shall humble himself shall be exalted.

This is consistent with what James wrote in his epistle:

Humble yourselves in the sight of the Lord, and he shall lift you up. (4:10)

On two other occasions, the disciples argued among themselves who would be the greatest. Jesus replied in Mark 9:35:

If any man desire to be first, the same shall be last of all, and servant of all.

In Luke 9:48, Jesus puts it this way:

For he that is least among you all, the same shall be great.

Clearly, there is a link between serving and being great. Leaders do well to remember this.

The Leader-Follower Link

When leaders remember to serve, they bring much from their days of following. Consider the forty years that Joshua served Moses. He was aide-de-camp for the leader of the children of Israel on their trek from captivity in Egypt to the Promised Land. Serving Moses, Joshua was a spy, a warrior, a minister, a mountain climber, and a close observer.

He did this for forty years! That is a long time to be serving, but it prepared him for what God had planned. Do you see his faithfulness in small things preparing him for bigger things? There are other examples:

- Joseph went from being a slave (Genesis 37:28) to number two in Egypt (41:40).
- David, the youngest in his family (1 Samuel 16:11), became king of Israel (2 Samuel 2:4).
- A captive in exile (Daniel 1:6), Daniel rose to the rank of first president in Babylon (6:2).
- Nehemiah, a lowly cupbearer (Nehemiah 1:11), was later governor (5:14).
- Orphaned Esther (Esther 2:7) became queen of Persia (2:17).

The best example is Jesus: from creator (John 1:3) to Savior (Acts 4:12) to the coming King (Revelation 19:16).

What do they all have in common? They were servants and followers before they were exalted, even the God-man, Jesus, who:

Took upon himself the form of a servant, and was made in the likeness of men: and being found in fashion as a man, he humbled himself, and became obedient unto death, even the death of the cross. Wherefore God also hath highly exalted him, and given him a name which is above every name. (Philippians 2:7b–9)

The link between serving and leading is well documented and unmistakable.

A Phone Call to San Antonio

In early 1999, I was stationed at Tinker Air Force Base in Oklahoma. I was on temporary duty in San Antonio, Texas, five hundred miles away, so I was in the right place at the right time when a medevac aircraft flew my wife, Karen, to the large military medical center there for surgery. Surgeons removed a giant cell tumor from her sacrum and inserted instrumentation to support that part of her spinal cord.

I balanced my work and family concerns well, working each day and visiting her each evening. Soon, however, the time came for her to return to Tinker to convalesce. I bid her good-bye as the medevac crew loaded her aboard the jet and flew away. I returned to my duties, five hundred miles from where she was going to be.

I really wrestled with this. I was uncomfortable being away from her when she needed me. It was my last thought before sleeping and the first in the morning.

I arrived at the office early the next day and one of my staff informed me I had just missed a call from my boss. I called him back immediately.

"What are you doing there?" he asked me.

I didn't understand the question; he knew exactly what I was doing. I was doing the job he had sent me to do.

He said that he knew that, but, "What are you doing there when your wife needs you here?"

It wasn't so much a question as a statement—an order. He told me to get on the next plane and he would find a replacement. He selected a close civilian friend of mine with whom I have remained close over the years. My two-star boss had shown his true servant colors.

To his own inconvenience and risk, he brought me back to Oklahoma. I was overwhelmed that he put my needs before his own. He, my boss, was the servant. Does that sound backward? It's not; it's the way it should be. Leaders serve. He took the initiative to do for me what was best, and he was willing to absorb the consequences to the mission. Good leaders do that—they serve even at their own peril. That general (no surprise) went on to a higher position and has been a mentor, friend, and confidant to me over the years.

Stop, Go

When I was a lieutenant colonel, I was the chief navigator in a C-130 flying squadron. We were flying high as a squadron (pun intended). We did everything well. We had a great leader as our commander. He inspired us, and we excelled—most of the time.

On one night training exercise, I was navigating along a course to a point where we would make the airdrop. I was sure I had the right position and called for the "green light" drop signal at the appropriate time. The paratroopers went out the door. Soon after they were all in the air, I saw the aim point still ahead of us, and the paratroopers landed well short of the drop zone. The results could have been worse, but that did little to assuage my sense of failure. Appropriately, I was decertified, retrained, took a check ride, and returned to my duties well bruised.

Soon after this humbling event, I moved to command a maintenance squadron. My squadron commander had looked beyond my misjudgment in one case and saw a leadership opportunity that would help the wing in another area. I had failed on one night and had to stop navigating, but there was a big "go" just around the corner. Instead of in operations, I was now in support. Though I didn't know it at the time, this change would take me to heights I would not have otherwise reached. My commander served the wing and this former chief navigator, who was now his peer and fellow squadron commander.

Serving is often better understood after the fact. Consider the mundane duties of a lieutenant who keeps track of flight publications or the sometimes boring duties of a tower officer.

Consider Joseph, David, Daniel, Nehemiah, and Esther in the Bible. Consider a phone call and a bad airdrop. Consider that the behind-the-scenes work you are doing now is both preparing you for the future but also demonstrating your real heart.

Some might say that an elevation in status sometimes comes to people other than servants. For example, royalty doesn't have to come up through the ranks (though monarchs do have to wait their "turn"), and some non-royal potentates misuse power in nonserving ways. But some present and future monarchs have found ways to serve their nation and people even before they ascend to the throne. Misusers of national power, however, who have little interest in serving, ultimately fail their people. I further observe that history ignores neither their means nor ends. As the Psalmist points out:

> The wicked walk on every side, when the vilest men
> are exalted. (Psalm 12:8)

The greatest is the servant, and he or she needs humility to balance two other leadership qualities that are apparent opposites—justice and mercy.

Discussion Questions

1. Remembering the two lieutenants who served their way to the top, what actions and what attitudes set them apart from their peers?
2. What do you think causes a leader "at the top" to stop serving? Can you cite an example of someone who did this? What was the result?
3. What is counterintuitive about a leader being a servant?
4. Tell about a leader you know who served before he or she was "in charge" and after. What strength(s) did a

servant's heart add to the leader's effectiveness?

5. What is gained by a leader spending time following? What biblical and nonbiblical examples of success are there in this?

6. In "A Phone Call to San Antonio," the leader showed great familiarity with the personal situation of a subordinate. What are things a leader can do to gain this insight?

7. What examples can you give of a person who came through a failure and went on to great things as a leader? What can we take away from that experience?

Two

SHOW JUSTICE, MERCY, AND HUMILITY

W hen I consider living the virtues of justice, mercy, and humility, the first words that come to mind are *conundrum* and *paradox*. Many questions follow: How does a leader be both just and merciful? Can they cohabitate, or are they mutually exclusive? What part does humility play in leadership, and what does it have to do with justice and mercy? Can a person be both a leader and humble? Should a leader exhibit justice, mercy, and humility, or should a leader demonstrate and value only one or two, but not all three? Those are fair questions.

Is Living All Three Possible?

A good place to start this discussion might be with a definition. According to the Free Dictionary website:

- *Justice* means "the principle of moral rightness; equity; conformity to moral rightness in action or attitude; righteousness."
- *Mercy* means "compassionate treatment, especially of those under one's power; clemency; a disposition to be kind and forgiving."
- *Humility* is a form of the word humble, which means, "marked by meekness or modesty of behavior, attitude, or spirit; not arrogant or prideful; showing deferential or submissive respect."

The first and last definitions use the word *attitude*, while the middle one uses *disposition*—both similar ideas. The first point, then, is that these actions flow from what is on the inside. A sense of justice compels actions that are just; it precipitates from the moral sense of rightness. And notice the recipient of the "compassionate treatment" in mercy: it is those whom the leader leads. Finally, a leader who acts humbly when others are watching but who isn't humble on the inside is just acting. The leader is fooled more often than the followers.

A second point in this discussion is the "and/or" question. I believe and have seen that effective leaders who master the third, can balance the first two. Leaders have to uphold standards—the principle of moral rightness. In the military, we call this "good order and discipline." It is essential for any organization's health and productivity, for its effectiveness. But I have also seen the wise leader who can balance the need for justice with compassion, "especially (with) those under one's power" or command. That leader can be firm in requiring the high standards but can also show mercy, even clemency on occasion. This comes easily from the meek one whose behavior, attitude, and spirit are modest (to hearken back to the definition), and who is comfortable being neither arrogant nor proud. Meekness has these attributes of humility in abundance; weakness doesn't.

Leaders can balance all three virtues and use them together, the first two strengthening each other in the presence of the third.

Who Says?

Of the more than thirty thousand verses in the Bible, I picked one many years ago as my favorite. To call it my life verse is to understate. It has encouraged me to live at a higher level than I would otherwise. It informs me what the Lord is expecting of me. And it comments on this matter of justice, mercy, and humility.

> He hath shown thee, O man, what is good: and what doth the Lord require of thee, but to do justly, and to love mercy, and to walk humbly with thy God. (Micah 6:8)

For starters, the three virtues are listed as what the Lord requires of us. That matters to me. Secondly, the word *and* joins the three together. That settles the "or" question: it is justice *and* mercy *and* humility.

Thirdly, we are to "do justly, and to love mercy." The one is an action that will flow from an attitude, and the other is an attitude that will flow to an action. When in doubt, do the right thing, but even then have a disposition to be kind and forgiving. Who says? The Lord says.

Here is the reality. It is easier to do justly *or* to love mercy than to do them together. It is easier to separate them than to combine them. Too often, leaders believe that justice and mercy are mutually exclusive, that it presents a dilemma. To uphold justice means you cannot be merciful, they believe, and if you show mercy, you are ignoring justice and letting the guilty get away with something. But the Bible instructs otherwise. Good leaders will practice both justice and mercy, and I have found that true, inward humility helps a leader to do so.

Scope of Application

I need to add just a few words about the scope of leading with both justice and mercy. It is easy for those high in an organization to see the applicability of this to those below and vice versa. It is the finger-pointing thing: remember, with one finger pointing outward, there are three pointing inward.

It applies to all levels in an organization and to leaders of all kinds. I have personally observed good and bad application in lots of leadership venues: teams, schools, churches, military, families, and businesses, and that means coaching, teaching, pastoring, commanding, parenting, and managing. You can add to this list. Exhibiting justice and mercy together applies to leading of all kinds.

Fasting and Weeping

Next to his slaying the giant, David's sin with Bathsheba is the best-known story of his lifetime. It is also the saddest. David was found out, confronted, and exposed.

Twice in 2 Samuel 12 we see justice, mercy, and humility playing out together. The first occurrence was when the prophet Nathan relays the Lord's message to David.

And David said unto Nathan, "I have sinned against the Lord." And Nathan said unto David, "The Lord also hath put away thy sin; thou shalt not die. Howbeit, because by this deed thou hast given great occasion to the enemies of the Lord to blaspheme, the child also that is born unto thee shall surely die." (vs. 13, 14)

David responded with humility by calling the sin what God called it—sin. Nathan indicated that God would not slay David; that was mercy. But Nathan continued that the Lord said the child would die—justice.

There are times when leaders must exact justice on one level but can give mercy on another. That is what happened with David.

Later, when the child became sick and died, David's servants didn't want to tell him the child had died. But David figured it out when he saw them whispering. He confronted them about it, and they confirmed what he suspected.

Then said his servants unto him, What thing is this that thou hast done? Thou didst fast and weep for the child, while it was alive: but when the child was dead, you didst rise and eat bread. And he said, While the child was yet alive, I fasted and wept: for I said, Who can tell whether God will be gracious to me, that the child may live? But now he is dead, wherefore should I fast? Can I bring him back again? I shall go to him, but he shall not return to me. (vs. 21–23)

For the second time in the same chapter, we see all three virtues—justice, mercy, and humility—knitted together. David fasted and wept—humility. He considered that God might be gracious to him—mercy. He acknowledged the death of his son—justice.

We also see examples of the three virtues occurring together in the New Testament.

Stoning and Writing

So many good things happen early in the morning. In his gospel, John records a story about a confrontation in chapter 8. Jesus had come from the Mount of Olives to the temple to teach the people "early in the morning."

> And the scribes and Pharisees brought unto him a woman taken in adultery; and when they had set her in the midst, they say unto him, Master, this woman was taken in adultery, in the very act. (vs. 3, 4)

They asked Him if they should stone her to death, as Moses had commanded. Their purpose was to gain something with which they could accuse Him. He responded in humility, justice, and mercy. The first thing Jesus did was:

> He stooped down, and with his finger wrote on the ground, as though he heard them not. (vs. 6)

That was an act of humility. We don't know what he wrote on the ground, but we see humility in his posture, and He didn't lash out at them. Recall the definition of *humility*. His response was one of "modesty of behavior, attitude, or spirit; not arrogant or prideful." He showed deference if not respect. Next, He addressed the justice of the dilemma.

> So when they continued asking him, he lifted up himself, and said unto them, He that is without sin among you, let him first cast a stone at her. (vs. 7)

He acknowledged the sin—that was justice. He didn't let her off without consequence. Instead, he said the sinless one among them should cast the first stone.

> And they which heard it, being convicted by their own
> conscience, went out one by one, beginning at the eld-
> est, even unto the last. (vs. 9)

They all left because none was without sin. In fact, Jesus
was the only sinless One among them, and He paid the price
for her sin later by dying for her sins and for the sins of her
accusers. He further showed his mercy when He spoke to her:

> Woman, where are those thine accusers? Hath no man
> condemned thee? She said, no man, Lord. And Jesus
> said unto her, Neither do I condemn thee: go, and sin
> no more. (vs. 10b, 11)

More mercy but a reminder of justice: "Go and sin no
more." The humble One perfectly balanced justice and mercy.
So should the aspiring leader.

Thank You

A close friend, fellow general officer, and former commander
related to me the following, which shows the balance between
justice and mercy.

> We "do justice" when we act appropriately to correct
> people and organizations who have not met standards
> or performed adequately. There is nothing in so acting
> that keeps us from caring for people involved and
> showing them mercy, understanding, and even love. I
> have given Article 15s [military administrative discipli-
> nary actions] where the person involved actually
> thanked me…not for the reduction in rank or the fine,

but for really meaning to use it as a rehabilitative tool, necessary for the unit's health but intended to uplift and constructively correct the person.

This general had a nice commander's touch, the touch of an effective leader. He understood the balance necessary. He upheld the needs of the organization and cared for the needs of the individual. In balancing both, he modeled justice and mercy. I also know him to model humility.

Deliberating Overnight

Because of my position of responsibility, at times I faced very important decisions. Some of them affected the lives of people and their families. I took these decisions seriously. Some decisions I just had to get right, and to make them hastily reduced the odds of that.

As a rule, the more important the decision, the longer I took to make it. There were often subordinates or supporting staff who had interest in a swift decision, but I stuck to my guns.

In the Air Force, when I had to make people decisions about administrative, nonjudicial, and court martial actions, I was deliberate and thorough. More often than not, I deliberated overnight or over many nights. I read all the pertinent material and talked with the right people. I listened. I moved its priority ahead of other things. I did everything I could to make the right decision.

Ensuring justice and balancing mercy requires humility to get it just right. It is something a leader does carefully.

Maintainer to Cop

On a visit to an airbase in Afghanistan, I arrived in time for supper. At the dining facility, (we no longer use the term *mess hall*) before I went through the serving line, I walked around the room and shook hands with each of the forty or so airmen, asking each his or her name, home unit, and job at the airbase.

I moved along at a good pace with brief exchanges, realizing I was holding them back from eating. About halfway through, a master sergeant said to me, "You saved my career." That was all. He gave no name or home base, and he said nothing about his job, as the others had done. I searched his eyes, then I glanced down at the nametag over his right breast pocket, but it rang no bells. He was smiling, but I could not place him and had no idea what he meant by, "You saved my career."

Then this veteran of eighteen or so years told me his story. Many years earlier, he was a technical training student at Sheppard Air Force Base in Texas, where I was a group commander. He had failed two progress tests in a crew chief training program and was being recommended for discharge from the Air Force. If I signed off on his package, he would be honorably discharged and sent home.

He related how I had asked his NCO (noncommissioned officer) to talk with him, and that I had subsequently transferred him into a security forces program at another base. Obviously, he had prospered in that field because he was now a senior noncommissioned office.

While I didn't remember his particular case, I know that I always gave such cases careful deliberation and frequently talked with the individual, not depending on the documentation alone. In this man's case, I balanced justice (eliminating him from a program he couldn't complete successfully) and mercy (finding another one where he could excel).

A few weeks after returning home from this trip, the man's mother sent me a letter saying how glad her son had been to be able to say thank you after all these years and how proud his entire family was that he was a senior NCO in the Air Force and now serving in Afghanistan. Her letter was a touching reminder to me to "do justly, and love mercy, and to walk humbly" with God.

Red Gym Bag

In the summer of 1971, my college basketball team travelled for some games in the Far East: Japan, Hong Kong, Taiwan, and the Philippines. I had already graduated, but the coach took me along for the trip. One day in Osaka, Japan, we were on a crowded train headed back to our quarters after a workout at an available gymnasium. I had a very nice red leather gym bag that held my size-12 Converse All-Star sneakers and other practice gear. There was little spare space on the train, so I put the gym bag on a rack over my head. We sped through the train system stop-after-stop.

Well into one stop, above the din of the crowd and announcements in Japanese, one of our group realized that this was our stop and shouted that we needed to get off the train before the doors closed. We scampered out of the train and we were relieved to see that we all had made it. Then the train accelerated away with my red gym bag still on the overhead rack.

In those days, finding size 12 sneakers in Japan wouldn't be easy. It would be infinitely easier to retrieve my gym bag. But the train disappeared out of sight. I prayed and asked the Lord to bring my red gym bag back to me. I told the coach I'd be right back, so he and the team waited there on the platform. I took the stairs two or three at a time on a dead run toward the stationmaster's small cluttered office in the heart of the station.

As best I could, saying "please" and "thank you" in Japanese, with the occasional "hi" (yes), and much gesturing, I explained the problem. He unrolled scrolls of what looked like architectural drawings and train schedules. He traced a circuitous path with his finger, looked me in the eye, dropped everything, checked his watch, and signaled for me to follow. I could hardly keep up. You see, that same train was returning and would be on a different level in only a few minutes.

Reaching the right level, I crouched down on my haunches and looked up through the windows as the slowing train arrived back in the station. I was looking for my red gym bag on an overhead rack. There it was. I accelerated down the platform as the train decelerated to keep up with the right car. When it stopped, I darted in one door, grabbed the gym bag, and rushed out another door before it closed, breathing, "Thank you, Lord." I'm sure the riders had some special thoughts, if not amusement, at seeing all of this.

I deserved justice for not being mindful enough to grab my bag on the way out of the train the first time. But I received mercy when the Lord literally brought the train back for me. In humility, I had asked for the impossible.

For the rest of the trip, team members frequently asked, "Hey, Loren, do you have your gym bag?" That was more justice!

Humility is a vital part of leadership. It plays out in the hearts of servants as they seek to serve. (Appendix A lists characteristics that show what humility looks like in flesh and blood.)

Discussion Questions

1. If justice and mercy are at the two ends of a continuum, what is at the other end of the continuum from humility?

2. Are justice and mercy really at opposite ends of a continuum? Can a leader do both in the same situation? Why or why not?

3. "Leaders can balance all three and use them together, the first two strengthening each other in the presence of the third." Do you agree or disagree with this statement? If you agree, how are the first two strengthened?

If you disagree, what influence, if any, does humility have on the other two?

4. Is the Micah 6:8 "and" argument compelling? Why or why not?

5. In what situations might you take Jesus' lead with an accuser by pretending to ignore the question or by just not answering?

6. What decisions in the vocation you are choosing or have chosen deserve overnight deliberation?

7. How far do you see the consequences of personnel decisions going? Cite an example of where this turned out for the good and another that turned out not so good. What do you take away from this?

8. In what situation have you had an experience like the red gym bag story? What was the key point in your story that turned it to a success or a failure?

THREE

SEEK TO SERVE

"WELL, OF COURSE I'D HELP IF YOU REALLY NEEDED IT."

The best leaders I have known not only serve when they have the opportunity, but they look for opportunities to serve. To do this does not come naturally; it takes work, observation, understanding yourself, and the right attitude about others. A close friend, Lt. Gen. (USAF, Ret.) Chris Miller, told me "the verb 'serve' is best (used) with a direct object. We serve a mission, a purpose, or a person. I have always been taught and (have) taught that the object of a leader's service can be anything but himself."

I couldn't agree more. In this context, seeking to serve has two elements.

Serving

As with many aspects of leading, it seems counterintuitive to suggest that leaders also serve. On the surface, these two actions seem to be opposites, but serving is part of leading.

There are at least two reasons why a leader who serves will find his or her stock rising. First, serving provides insight into one's organization and the needs of the people he or she leads. It's a way to keep in touch with the mission and the people. Serving enables the leader to experience firsthand what those lower in the organization see and do and what they need and feel. It helps the leader identify with those he or she seldom or never sees, and it lets the followers see the leader up close. I cannot overstate the benefit of serving to the mission and the people.

A second reason for serving is that it sets a positive example. The second Air Force core value is service before self. Putting others before oneself strengthens organizations, and there is no better way to promulgate it than for the leader model it. What the boss thinks is important to others.

When I was a younger officer, I studiously paid attention to the questions my bosses asked and the things in which they showed interest. It gave me a glimpse into what they valued, and it helped me set my course. A leader's agenda should be important to subordinates, and a leader's boss's agenda may be even more important. A leader should set the example in areas he wants others to emulate, and serving is one of those.

There are biblical examples of leaders who serve in the lives of King David, Abigail, Joseph, Daniel, Joshua, and, of course, Jesus. There are more recent examples too. Consider why presidents rush to the site of a tragedy to comfort victims and their families. President Bush did this continually through his presidency, reaching out to the families of 9/11 victims, and President Obama has done similarly for families at Sandy Hook.

There are myriad other examples. Boy Scouts make community service part of their merit process. NCAA football teams take on the needs of groups or individuals in the community. College students sacrifice lucrative summer internships in favor of serving those who are in need. There are soup kitchens, places of refuge for the homeless like Chicago's Pacific Garden Mission, Goodwill, AM Vets, and so many others doing worthy service for those in need.

When I was in the Air Force, it was common for members of our squadrons to serve outside their normal duties. I have seen airmen serving with Big Brothers and Big Sisters of America, the American National Red Cross, the Boy Scouts of America, and along highways cleaning up trash.

Sometimes it's easier to serve outside the workplace than within it. Leaders who model serving in the workplace are apt to see an epidemic of sorts in serving—the good kind of epidemic. It strengthens the organization's performance and reputation, and it adds to a sense of accomplishment among the followers.

Serving is part of the formula that identifies future good leaders. Those who serve well today will likely lead well tomorrow. But serving should not end after placement in a leadership position. Leaders need to keep on serving.

I have a dear friend whose son requires significant medical and rehabilitative attention. He has made progress from the coma he was in some months ago. My friend is a senior executive with a prominent company, but he has taken the time necessary to be with his son every step of the way. I doubt he has any free time at all. While it is out of love, he has modeled serving to all who watch: those at his workplace, those who follow the story of God's mercy and miracles online, and those fortunate enough to be his friend. He is a giant among leaders because of how he serves.

Seeking

Serving is one thing, but seeking to serve is another. To look for opportunities to serve is quite different from serving when opportunities present themselves. The former tells of one's attitude, the latter of one's willingness. Doing what others ask or suggest is beneficial and commendable; doing what others need but have not asked for is something else entirely.

Not everyone sees the opportunities that exist around them. A leader has to work at seeking to serve. Many see the piece of paper or crushed soda can beside the sidewalk, but only those seeking to serve will step aside to pick it up. Many will hear of the death or hospitalization of a family member, but only those who seek to serve will insist on bringing over a meal to the grieving family or organize an effort that would provide it for a week.

I know a pastor who has mastered seeking to serve. When there has been even a small, barely noticeable need in my life, he has sprung into action to meet it, to ask about it, to pray for it, and to follow up days or even weeks later by asking about it. He is a young man and very mature in this area. He would credit his wife as being the one who so keenly seeks to serve others. This is no surprise to me.

Seeking to serve takes serving to a new level that will prosper a leader's organization.

The Good Samaritan

A certain lawyer was having a conversation with Jesus one day. The lawyer asked, "Who is my neighbor?" The subsequent story in Luke 10:30-37 is one of the best known in the Bible. Its hero, the Good Samaritan, has become such a standard for seeking to serve that hospitals sometimes use the expression, or part of it, in their names.

Let me summarize. A man on a trip was attacked, probably robbed, stripped of his clothes, wounded, and then abandoned. A religious leader came along, saw what had happened, and promptly passed by on the other side of the road. Another religious leader came along later and looked a little closer, but he also passed on the other side of the road.

When a man of a despised city and ethnic background came by, he chose to serve the abandoned victim. The Samaritan took many actions that day when the religious leaders had not taken even one—culminating in a promise to the innkeeper to repay whatever the bills totaled. Amazing.

There was ample opportunity for the first two more logical passers-by to assist, but they refused. A third, less-likely helper came by and, seeking to serve, jumped in with both feet. It wasn't on the schedule for the day, but he did it anyway. It probably made him late for a meeting, but he judged it a higher priority. In fact, it became the purpose for the day. Like a good leader, he did hand off the man's care to the innkeeper so he could continue his journey, late, no doubt. And with the delegation, he also committed to follow up later. This is the perfect model of seeking to serve.

I offer one other observation. We know more about the two who didn't serve than we do of the one who did. We don't know his name, occupation, or destination. We don't know his age, family size, or financial status. There is no indication that he was religious. This is often the case with those who seek to serve. They are more interested in the service than in getting the credit for it.

Stephen

The early church had a need to care for widows. Like then, today we have widows and orphans all around us. Early church leaders decided to do something about the need. They valued this work so much that they set pretty high qualification criteria for those they selected. According to Acts 6:2–5, they sought men who were honest, full of the Holy Ghost, wise, and full of faith. Stephen was one such man, along with six others. He was well educated, articulate, bold, and powerful. Later, it was Stephen whom the local Jewish leaders in Jerusalem targeted as a blasphemer. After they arrested him and suborned witnesses to testify falsely against him, they stoned him to death.

It is interesting to note that Stephen was a servant while he was leading. On the one hand, you might say that it didn't end well for him. But the cause of his life—the church—flourished because of his sacrifice. He was true to the end and a model for leaders today.

After the Game

When I was a young officer, I heard stories about a lieutenant colonel squadron commander in Europe who had subsequently risen to the highest military position in the United States. He was special long before he was prominent.

This flying squadron commander would come to little league baseball games to watch his son play. After the game, he and his son would walk around the bleachers and even under them to pick up all the trash the other parents and spectators had left on the ground. You know what this would be like— dirty paper with mustard stains, sticky soda cans, and bubble gum on the soles of shoes.

There was no one to see, but that wasn't the purpose for what he was doing. He wanted to leave the ballpark better than he found it. The cleanup didn't take long, and he was modeling seeking to serve to his son. I don't know what effect it had on his son, but the word of such humble service followed him throughout his career and fell on the ears of this young lieutenant an ocean away. Such is often the outcome of seeking to serve.

I'll Get It

What that squadron commander did had an impact on me. I remembered it through my entire career. Because of his example, coupled with the aversion aircrews have for trash on the ground, I seldom walked by litter without picking it up.

One time when I was walking around the outside of the largest building at an air logistics center, I saw more than a little trash in the grass. Though there were several people walking with me, I bent over to pick up the first item. Moments later, I picked up another without breaking the conversation at all. When I came to the third item only steps later, one of those with me said, "I'll get it."

On the rest of the walk, before I came to an item on the ground, one of my subordinates rushed ahead to retrieve it. I was doing more than picking up trash, I was teaching them to seek to serve.

Midnight Chili

Once my first sergeant and I made chili and cornbread at midnight and served it to our squadron. Nothing like that had ever been done in that unit. I'm not sure if it was the first sergeant's or my idea, but it was a good one. We were seeking to serve.

There is a postscript. The first sergeant made the cornbread, and I made the chili. I had never made chili before, or if I had, certainly never in that large of a quantity. I used a large canning pot—probably a three-gallon size—and prepared the chili at home.

It was easy to brown the hamburger meat, to pour in the diced tomatoes and sauce, and to add the chopped onions. No beans—it was to be Texas chili! Then how hard would it be to add the cayenne pepper? If a little would be good, more would be better, so in went the whole can. When that was finished, the chili bubbled and was finally ready for the squadron.

The first sergeant and I served the men and women from both the swing shift that ended at midnight and the grave shift that started at that time. All went well at the start. The first airmen to sample the chili responded quickly to the pepper. It didn't take them long to figure out that the pepper temperature was, shall we say, excessive.

Discreetly, they found their way to the bathrooms, flushed the chili, and then proudly brought their empty bowls back for the first sergeant's praise. He wasn't impressed when he figured out what had happened and insisted that each airman get back in line for a second serving. He wasn't going to let his commander be embarrassed.

He and I laughed about the midnight chili for years to come. We were two leaders just seeking to serve.

Mister President

During the Presidents' Day holiday in February 2001, a month after he took office, I had the privilege of meeting President George W. Bush on the ramp at Tinker Air Force Base. He had flown in Air Force One to Oklahoma City and was using the base as his arrival and departure point to support him as he made a speech downtown.

Along with the mayor of Oklahoma City, the commander of the air logistics center, our senior civilian, and our wives, we were the short receiving line to greet the President and First Lady on their arrival. We had been instructed not to engage him in conversation but just to greet him with something cordial. In the few days before we knew of the visit, I thought about what I would say to the most powerful man in the world in the few seconds I would have.

The President and First Lady walked briskly down the stairs

of the large VC-25 Boeing 747 aircraft with smiles on their faces. They were obviously happy to be in Oklahoma City. The Secret Service was positioned close enough to react if necessary but far enough back to give the President room to move down the receiving line.

He was with the mayor, then with my boss. Karen and I were next in line. The First Lady preceded him. After she moved to Karen and then on down the line, he stepped right into my space—up close. I said with a deep breath, "Mr. President, I pray for you."

He had just finished shaking my hand and was ready to release it and move on, but he turned back. He moved in even closer. So did the Secret Service. He then told me some things that indicated to me that he valued people praying for him and the privilege of serving the people of the United States. He was genuinely appreciative.

Politics aside, I am certain that on that day, less than seven months before an event that would change his presidency and our nation forever, he was seeking to serve, and he valued one airman praying for him. (It had been my custom for years to pray for my chain of command and "For kings [presidents] and for all that are in authority". (1 Timothy 2:2a))

Tough "Call"

In an earlier chapter, I wrote of the time my boss brought me back to Tinker Air Force Base in Oklahoma City from San Antonio, Texas. He truly showed his servant colors. There was another aspect to that story.

When I bid my wife good-bye, I was struggling inwardly with my priorities. Should I remain in Texas serving my boss and the important work I was leading, or should I return to Oklahoma to serve my wife in her need? There would be consequences, no doubt, if I asked to be relieved from my duty in

Texas, but I became willing to absorb these if necessary in favor of my lifelong relationship with my wife. I resolved to call my two-star general commander the following morning. It was going to be a tougher call than it should have been.

I arrived at the office early the next day. As I was looking up my boss's phone number, one of my staff stuck his head into the office to inform me I had just missed my boss's call. I called him back immediately. I told him I was returning his call but that I was on the brink of calling him anyway.

My dilemma had been between serving my boss and serving my wife. I chose to do the latter. It was gratifying to me to know that my boss had come to the same conclusion, though I knew this wouldn't always be the case. That day, I found that my choice in seeking to serve was closely connected to my priorities, and that is why I chose for Karen.

There was no adverse consequence for me. In retrospect, I think it impressed or at least pleased the general that I put my family ahead of my own advancement.

This story gives a hint of another quality of leadership. Seeking to serve requires selflessness; so does sharing credit and shouldering blame.

Discussion Questions

1. How are serving and seeking to serve different?
2. Can seeking to serve be taken to an extreme? Can serving be taken to an extreme? What are examples and the results of each?
3. What example have you seen where a modern-day Good Samaritan went as far as the biblical one did? Of all he did, what one action stands out to you above the others?
4. Stephen and his six compatriots were very well qualified, yet they were picked only to be servants—to wait

tables. Do servants need to be so well qualified? If so, why? If not, what is the point of the story?

5. In the vocation you are choosing or have chosen, besides being an example, how will you teach others to serve and to seek to serve? If you have had success in this or witnessed it in others, how did it look?

6. How do you recover from too much cayenne pepper in the chili of life? Should the commander have asked his wife to prepare the chili? In other words, should leaders get their hands dirty by doing real work or should they live above the fray?

7. If you had a moment alone with the president of the United States, what would you say or ask him? If a person well below you in the organizational chain told you one thing, what would you want it to be? Name something someone has said to you that had real impact, whether good or bad.

8. What criteria would you use in choosing between two service opportunities or responsibilities?

FOUR

SHARE CREDIT, SHOULDER BLAME

Some of the other actions we have covered are easier than this one. This one gets to the heart of the leader. Like seeking to serve, this one reveals on the outside what is going on in the inside. No matter the difficulty or consequences, good leaders share the credit and shoulder the blame.

Credit

Many times, too many to count, individuals came into my office with the following report: "I have some good news." Fewer times, savvy intermediaries brought subordinates with this report: "Why don't you tell General Reno what you and your team did?" I endured the former and loved the latter.

The focus of the first was on the reporter, the *I*, though I knew the person was just reporting what others had done. Seldom does a single person make something significant happen. Think of Doolittle's Raid, the first man on the moon, and the Normandy Invasion. They were armies of men and women doing the work—and the third one literally!

Even smaller successes are usually the work a few visible people and a lot of people behind the scenes. Sharing the credit brings to light those who work in darkness as well those who work in the limelight. In the Air Force, launching a jet aircraft was little the pilot's doing and much the doing of the maintainers. Some of the maintainers were doing their part during the midnight shift, literally in the darkness.

Because hierarchies are what they are, the few often get credit for the work of many. I beamed one day at the Pentagon when the chief of staff was praising several maintainers for being the best in the Air Force. When it was his turn to speak, the first award recipient immediately gave credit to those who worked with him, his supervisor, and the leadership of his commander. Right off the flight line and now standing in the presence of the Air Force's most senior leaders, he exemplified one thing that leaders do: share the credit.

When the second recipient received her award, she did exactly the same. And so it went right down the line. Each of these Best in the Air Force winners shared the credit with others who weren't even present. It's no wonder the Air Force maintainers are so cherished—officers, NCOs, and airmen alike.

If it's a small success, leaders look to recognize small teams. If it's a huge success, it's usually a large team that did it, and to think one individual alone was responsible is nearsighted. Look for the team or remember the team, and share the credit.

Blame

While not sharing the credit can happen due to a loss of awareness in a moment of delight, not shouldering the blame usually happens because of a more deeply rooted issue. It is usually a person not wanting to be seen as a failure who loses focus and is not ready for the next step.

It is amazing how much some people think about tomorrow's opportunities but fail to take care of today's business. The batter who is thinking about how loud the crowd will cheer when he knocks it out of the park is more likely to hear the thump in the catcher's mitt than to connect with the ball.

Misappropriating credit says, "I have some good news"; not shouldering the blame says, "We have a problem." To be sure, problems need a team approach, but leaders need to own the problems and then lead the solutions.

I heard a senior military leader whom I know well and respect highly tell a group of US Senators recently that he had taken his eye off the ball but that he would fix the matter; it was his to do. He was taking ownership of the problem and shouldering the blame. In fact, the problem started off his watch, but he never even hinted of that. He showed his broad shoulders that day.

As the contributions to a success are usually the work of many, the failures are usually attributable to a few. Good leaders understand this, and they look below the surface to recognize the worthy in each case. If the recognition is for good, they reward publicly; if not, then they usually reprimand privately.

Recognition for doing well usually flows more easily than does recognition for doing wrong. It seems that many leaders are more comfortable complimenting than confronting. Some step away from association with a problem, mishap, or failure. True leaders step right up.

I recently took my car to a garage to have the oil changed. It had been almost exactly 5,000 miles, and it was time. When I received the car back, the service manager proudly told me the car was ready. He was so amiable that I later thought he was hoping I'd remember his name when I was asked to fill out a survey. He hadn't done the work, but he was more than ready to receive the credit.

When I seated myself behind the wheel to drive away, I noticed two things: the decal reminder on the windshield showed a return in 4,000 miles, not 5,000, and there was an oily footprint and other oily scuffs on the driver's-side floor mat. I mentioned both to the service manager. He corrected the former and half-corrected the latter.

When he called a day later inquiring about the service, I reminded him of the two problems. He replied, "I'm sorry you feel that way." How would you grade this response? An A-plus response would have been, "I'm sorry we didn't treat you better," or, "That was my fault entirely. Please let me make it up to you." Effective leaders share the credit and shoulder the blame.

Some Problems Are Giants

We all know the story of David and Goliath, the Israelites and the Philistines, the boy and the giant. You may have heard the children's song about "only a boy named David" and "five little stones he took." David understood and lived this principle of sharing the credit, even as a young man facing a giant.

After David rejected the king's armor, he went to stand before the giant. Goliath thundered:

"Am I a dog that thou comest to me with staves?" And the Philistine cursed David by his gods. And the Philistine said to David, "Come to me, and I will give thy

flesh unto the fowls of the air, and to the beasts of the
field." (1 Samuel 17:43–44)

I wouldn't say Goliath lacked confidence. He was fully confident in his ability to win this fight! Let's consider this matter
of confidence, for David's was in something else.

Then said David to the Philistine, "Thou comest to me
with a sword, and with a spear, and with a shield: but
I come to thee in the name of the Lord of hosts, the
God of the armies of Israel, whom thou hast defiled."
(vs. 45)

These words probably didn't faze Goliath. They should
have, and they are the beginning of the last words he would hear
before literally losing his head over the matter. David said before
the battle that he came not in his own strength, armor, and confidence, but in the "name of the LORD of hosts."

David said this when he was still far off, so he must have
shouted it. Note in verse 48 that Goliath arose to meet David
and that David ran to meet him. There had to be some distance
between them. Does this mean that some or perhaps all of the
Israelite army heard David's proclamation? I think so.

David gave the credit to the Lord of hosts, and he did it
before the battle. It is easier to share the credit after an under-
taking than before it because you don't know the outcome
beforehand. David was confident that the Lord would deliver
the giant. The Lord still delivers us from giants of all kinds.

David shared the credit; a successor shouldered the blame.

Cupbearer to Governor

Nehemiah was a cupbearer to an ancient king of Persia. The
cupbearer was either a deported citizen of a conquered nation

or the son of one. He was a high official with access to the potentate, the all-powerful king.

Some of Nehemiah's countrymen came to him and told him how their homeland lay in ruins, and the people were "in great affliction and reproach" (Nehemiah 1:3).

What a leader Nehemiah was! Hearing the news, he "sat down and wept, and mourned certain days, and fasted and prayed before the God of heaven" (vs. 4).

The best is still to come. So far, he has shown his emotion and devotion to his homeland and his people. But notice how he shoulders the blame. Over the span of less than two verses, he owns the problem that caused the captivity and ruin in a prayer to the commander's Commander-in-Chief:

> (I) confess the sins of the children of Israel, which we
> have sinned against thee: both I and my father's house
> have sinned. We have dealt very corruptly against thee.
> (vs. 6, 7)

Three times he takes the blame. God can use leaders like this, and He used this man. Nehemiah took a promotion and change of assignment to become a traveler, then a builder, then a general, then the governor, and then probably back to the service of the king. Leaders who shoulder the blame are ready for bigger things.

My Fault

I was a newlywed husband in 1976 and took my bride, Karen, back to my base of assignment, Clark Air Base, in the Republic of the Philippines. I was a young C-130 navigator. Within days of arriving home after our honeymoon in the United States, I was assigned to fly in a formation of nine aircraft.

The flight profile called for me to navigate the number 2

aircraft in close formation, following the lead aircraft at 300 feet above the ground at nearly 300 miles per hour, pop up to 1,100 feet as we approached the drop zone (DZ), and release a pallet of heavy equipment that would float down under parachutes to the aim point on the DZ. Then the plane was to accelerate, descend, and we would return to our base—all in formation with the other eight aircraft. The DZ was at the north end of the base, though the flight would take us some 200 miles around the island of Luzon before dropping our load.

After we completed our aircrew briefing at the squadron briefing room, we headed out to the aircraft. I had just enough time before catching the crew transport to give Karen a call and tell her the time and place where she could watch what her new husband did. I explained that I would be in the number 2 aircraft—right behind the formation leader. I was nearly as excited as she was in knowing that she would be watching.

The day progressed exactly as planned. We arrived at the aircraft and completed the preflight of all the equipment at the same time as the other eight aircrews. We all started engines at exactly the same time, as briefed. We began our taxi to the main runway at precisely the same moment. What a sight that must have been. We called it an "elephant walk"—nine large aircraft lumbering along slowly at a walking pace through the hardstand parking spaces and onto the parallel taxiway. We were all lined up in the right sequence. I was right behind the leader.

We taxied into position on the active runway, awaiting clearance for takeoff from the tower. When cleared, we powered the engines and lifted off to our assembly altitude. We joined into formation and tightened it up so every aircraft was in the right position. Then something unexpected happened.

We were flying this formation in practice for an inspection that was only weeks away. Accordingly, there was a flight evaluator on the lead aircraft. He handed the pilot a short note that said something like, "Simulate you have been hit with AAA fire, break out of the formation, and return to base." Do you have the picture? With number 1 gone, number 2 is now in the lead.

But I was ready for the challenge. I had carefully drawn and studied the route we were to fly. I knew what landmarks to look for: the terrain features, river bends, small towns, towers, and the road intersections. I knew what time we were to be at each checkpoint and the heading we were to take on the next leg. I was ready, pumped, and on top of every detail. I was ready to lead.

It went well all the way around the route. We were less than 5 seconds early or late at each point when 30 seconds would have been satisfactory. We kept closing in on the target, and it looked like we'd be either exactly on time or no more than 2 seconds off. Incredible. And the formation was coming right behind me.

We approached the DZ from the north. When it was in sight, we called on the radio for drop clearance from the controlling agency. There was no answer. We called a second time. Again, there was no answer. When there was no answer the third time, we began to prepare for a no-drop and escape from the DZ, per our special instructions. But as we peered toward the DZ, only a few miles and half as many minutes ahead, we saw from the DZ aim point green smoke that was laying down close to the ground moving from left to right.

If the smoke had been red, it would be the signal for a no-drop. But since it was green, that was as good as the verbal clearance, so we proceeded inbound. Having aced the first part of the flight, I was confident as I directed the pilot to position our aircraft to the right of the DZ so our load would move right along the smoke and end where the smoke began—a perfect bull's-eye.

Because the smoke was blowing to the right, I thought our

load would move to the left. Do you see the same logic I saw? I doubt it! Neither did the very experienced pilot, but I talked him out of his suggestions. The co-pilot was more adamant, but I convinced him, too. The flight engineer who was watching the whole picture piled on with the other two, but I prevailed. When we were nearly abeam and well right of the aim point, I called, "Green light," the signal for the loadmaster to let the load fly. And fly it did.

The rest of the formation appropriately flew down the left side of the DZ. Judging that the wind that was causing the smoke to lay low close to the ground was strong, they gave plenty of room for the load to drift to the right and land where it was intended. It did exactly as they planned—seven bull's-eyes.

Predictably, my load landed well off the drop zone to the right, off the reservation, and was unrecoverable in the jungle. What is the point of this story? It is my culpability. I was at fault.

I made the initial mistake in logic. I ignored three would-be helpers: the pilot, co-pilot, and flight engineer. I also called the green light, so there was no other person to blame. I was not being magnanimous in accepting this blame; I deserved it. It was time to shoulder the blame for what I had done in leading my crew astray.

Sometimes we think leaders are being disingenuous in shouldering the blame, but Nehemiah and the leaders I know who have done this noble deed have done it with sincerity. That is what makes them worthy leaders and ready for more responsibility. Saying it and saying it with feeling are two different things. The latter is better.

Ice Cream Discount

I used to make frequent trips through the Lambert-St Louis International Airport. It's a grand airport terminal, and the mural on the lower level continues to captivate me.

I was traveling in my Air Force uniform one day and went to get some ice cream. I saw the prices, and the one I wanted cost three dollars and some change. I was surprised when the server said I owed two dollars and some change. My integrity is worth more than a dollar!

I corrected her and said the correct amount, reading right off the sign. She told me they gave the airline pilots a discount, and since I was an airline pilot, she just gave me the discount without saying so. I tried to give her the full amount, explaining I wasn't an airline pilot but in the Air Force. She said, "Airlines, Air Force, it's all the same to me." She sure was sharing the credit.

Signal to Eat

From the time our children were small, we taught them the importance of honoring the person who prepared the meals we ate. It was our family tradition not to take a bite of the meal until the preparer did first. While our daughter was too young to understand all the mechanics, I helped her by telling her that I'd just nod when it was time for her to begin eating.

This arrangement worked fine for a couple of years. Once at a dinner with guests, I forgot to nod to her and engaged in an interesting adult conversation. My four-year old sat to my left and kept her hands on her lap. She gazed up into my eyes while tears streamed down her cheeks. Part way through the meal, I noticed her just sitting there and immediately knew my mistake. It was time for me to shoulder the blame for what I had not done in leading my daughter.

We changed the procedure after my heartrending apology to my daughter. From then on, when I took a bite, she was cleared to eat! That worked fine for her and her two younger brothers through their childhood.

No Show

One of my Air Force assignments included mentoring about a dozen young captains who were hand-selected for a special assignment. We called them CBOs, career broadening officers.

My wife invited the CBOs over to the house for an evening of food and fun. They all sent an RSVP indicating that they would come. This was no surprise, given that our relationship was one of mutual affection and respect. The evening started and ended nicely except that one young officer and his wife did not come. I found it a little strange because he had indicated he would be there.

It turned out he just forgot. (I have done the same thing more than once.) When I arrived at the office at 6:30 the next morning, he was already there. I have no idea how long he had been waiting. He was wearing his service dress uniform, reported in formally, and gave me a lengthy, well-rehearsed apology for missing the event. But he made no excuse. He told me he had just forgotten and asked if I would forgive him.

There are a dozen reasons he could have used, and I would never have known. Instead he came completely clean, did it early the following morning, and completely shouldered the blame. He didn't worry that I might think less of him; he just 'fessed up.

I thought more of him for the way he handled this than if he had attended the event. I saw him a dozen years later, and he was prospering in his career, which was no surprise. We talked about it and both laughed. What character he demonstrated at such an early stage in his career. He understood the importance of shouldering the blame.

Shouldering the blame takes courage, and so does asking for help when you need it.

Discussion Questions

1. Have you seen a leader truly share the credit without taking a disproportionate share? Who was it, and what did it look like?

2. To what extent should a leader shoulder the blame for what others have done or not done?

3. How does it water down or even void an apology when someone says, "I'm sorry if you were offended by what I did." What are the elements of shouldering the blame without caveat?

4. David gave the Lord credit even before the battle with Goliath. Was this risky? Have you ever seen someone give credit before the accomplishment, and if so, what was the effect on others?

5. Did Nehemiah overreach in shouldering the blame for what others had done?

6. How far should a leader go in giving credit to a team when the credit-givers insist on praising the leader alone?

7. What are the merits in shouldering blame quickly? Have you or someone you know been in this situation? How did it play out?

8. What is behind a leader thinking more of a person for taking the blame than about the act of commission or omission that caused the issue?

9. What should a leader do and not do after shouldering the blame? Whom do you know who has done this well?

10. How can a leader share the credit beyond making a general announcement? Whom do you know who has done this well?

FIVE

ASK FOR HELP
WHEN YOU NEED IT

"NO. NO. I DOUBT IF YOU COULD HELP. IT'S A SOFTWARE GLITCH."

Most leaders are "type A" personalities. They are driven, dependable, self-reliant, and capable. They plow through obstacles when necessary or nimbly circumnavigate them. They do what it takes, and that is one of the reasons they are leaders. They are wired that way, and they have the track record to support the challenges incumbent with their responsibilities. Asking for help does not come naturally for them.

We All Need Help Sometimes

Despite the drive and determination most leaders possess, there are times when they need help. It can be because of the size, complexity, detail, or duration of a challenge.

Size: A leader will sometimes defer to subordinates choosing a course of action, knowing that they will better own the outcome than if the leader had chosen for them.

Complexity: Some problems are just beyond the expertise of the leader, so the leader relies on those who know everything about it. When this happens, a wise leader draws on those experts to gain their insight and also to send a signal that they are valued.

Detail: Some challenges are more detailed than time allows, so the leader again relies on others for the detail work. The leader depends on summaries, conclusions, and finished products. The leader may defer the details, but he or she follows the advice President Reagan once gave when negotiating nuclear disarmament with the Soviet Union: "Trust but verify."

Duration may also be a consideration in asking for help. Some projects are so protracted that the leader relies on incremental updates in lieu of hands-on involvement. At my last job in the Air Force, there was a very important issue that I needed to resolve, track, and inform my boss about. For nearly three years, I took updates every Friday morning on this matter, and we worked from a detailed plan with milestones and offices of primary responsibility who worked the issues through the weeks. Because of the project's duration, I delegated its leadership to others. But I stayed in the game weekly and kept my boss informed too.

Another scenario when a leader needs to ask for help is when he or she just doesn't know what to do or where to turn. This may be because the project is new to the leader or because there are too many unknowns. When I was in leadership positions, I cultivated a small circle of peers whom I trusted explicitly. They permitted me to approach them confidentially on any matter. Each of them also consulted me with the same considerations. I approached these respected men and women on important matters when I thought I was right but wanted a sounding board, a sanity check. These colleagues were invaluable to me. They were commanders from squadron to numbered air force levels, a director of logistics for a major command, fellow deputy chiefs of staff at the Pentagon, a defense agency director, and others.

It's a two-way street: good leaders need to ask for help sometimes, and they need to be ready to help others who might call on them.

Weakness or Meekness?

You may think that asking for help is a sign of weakness. Leaders make things happen, plow through obstacles, and are wired to live above the fray. Well, sort of, but not exactly.

Asking for help is less a sign of weakness than of meekness. You know the meaning of the former; the latter means strength under control. Asking for help shows humility. It is an acknowledgment that one is not omnipotent or omniscient. The only One who has both of those attributes is available for us too. Consider the following:

> If any of you lack wisdom, let him ask of God, that giveth to all men liberally, and upbraideth not; and it will be given him. (James 1:5)

From a practical perspective, I have also observed that there is value, not harm, in asking for help. I worked for a four-star commander who gave me great latitude in my job but who was always available. On one occasion, he offered to weigh in on a matter with which I was wrestling. He was sure, though not in an arrogant way, that he could achieve the desired result quicker and easier than I could at my level. There was no doubt about that! But I needed to build a relationship that his intervention would have stalled. I thanked him for his offer but kept the action for myself.

The lesson I learned from this helpful and gracious leader was that I needed to be available to my subordinates, and that I could do that, be aware of their needs, and offer to help but not take over just because it suited me. There is always the commander's prerogative, but inserting oneself at will isn't always prudent. He did not impugn me for needing help, neither did he force himself into the situation. I never had any reservations about asking that commander for help.

Why in This Order?

The title of Chapter 3 was "Seek to Serve." It is not coincidental that seeking to serve comes before asking for help when you need it.

The first instinct of the two should be to serve. A leader at any level needs to think about serving, not asking for help all the time. If the leader never solves anything, never sets the course and pace, never shows accountability, never exercises, and never seeks to serve, he or she will likely be doing something different in short order. Serve first, but then ask for help if you need it.

The second instinct should be to ask for help when you need it. The strong leader will cultivate an environment where subordinates know they may ask for help. I do mean "may"— they have permission and don't need to fear recriminations. They don't have to make a formal request for permission to ask a question.

I worked for a boss once who didn't want to see anyone until he had read the newspaper and had a cup of coffee. When I occasionally had to ask him for help, I walked on eggshells.

Because of this experience, I decided I would go out of my way to keep the door open to superiors, peers, and subordinates alike.

Leaders who perfect seeking to serve also need to be able to ask for help when they need it.

Famine in the Land

There is a story within a story that I missed for some time. The larger story is about Joseph, who went from favorite son to slave to prisoner to prime minister. The embedded story is about his father, the great patriarch, Jacob, later called Israel.

We pick up the story after Joseph's coat of many colors, after his dreams, after he was sold to the merchants, and after his time in Potiphar's house, prison, Pharaoh's dreams, and Joseph's promotion to number two in the land of Egypt.

> Now when Jacob saw that there was corn in Egypt, Jacob said unto his sons, "Why do ye look one upon another?" And he said, "Behold, I have heard that there is corn in Egypt: get you down thither, and buy for us from thence: that we may live and not die." (Genesis 42:1, 2)

Let's look at the life of Jacob. He was a great patriarch, the grandson of Abraham, the son of Isaac. He was the father of 12 sons, not an insignificant fact given the culture and expected progeny. Consider the size of the present he planned for his brother, Esau: 200 female and 20 male goats, 200 female sheep and 20 rams, 30 milking camels with their colts, 40 cows and ten bulls, and 20 female donkeys and 10 colts (see 32:13-15). That was a present, not the entirety of his livestock! Consider that it took 10 of Jacob's grown sons and who knows how many servants to take only the flock to Shechem to feed them (see 37:1).

We are talking about a very wealthy man and a great leader, no doubt. He knew when he needed help, and he wasn't reluctant to ask for it. He told his sons to go to Egypt to buy corn that they might "live and not die" (42:2).

It was a serious situation. He didn't send them because he thought he could get a better price. He wasn't playing the commodity market. It is apparent that he had worked all his own options. He sent them because he heard there was corn there. Obviously, there was none where he was.

After he exhausted his options but before it was too late, he dispatched his sons. Some subordinates wait until there is no time even for a powerful superior to snatch the bacon from the fire. Jacob waited, but only lead time away from starvation. In other words, he acted in time for them to go and return with food before they ran out. He needed help and he asked for it. So should we—civilian and military leaders alike.

The Centurion Asks for Help

One such military leader, an officer over 100 men, came to Jesus one day around 30 AD. The centurion had a very sick servant and needed help. The servant had palsy, which is defined as "complete or partial muscle paralysis, often accompanied by loss of sensation and uncontrollable body movements or tremors," according to the Free Dictionary website.

Consider one word in the story, told in Matthew 8:5-13, that I read past for years:

And when Jesus was entered into Capernaum, there came unto him a centurion, beseeching him. (vs. 5)

The word is *beseeching*. Too often we skip right past this word to get to the part about the centurion humbling himself and telling the Lord,

For I am a man under authority, having soldiers under me: and I say to this man, "Go," and he goeth; and to another, "Come," and he cometh; and to my servant, "Do this," and he doeth it. (vs. 9)

What does *beseeching* mean? The Free Dictionary website says it means to "ask someone urgently and fervently to do something; implore; entreat." This military officer—a commander—is not asking, but pleading for help. He wasn't doing this on the phone, by e-mail or text, or in a closed-door session. It was out in the open. He persistently asked for help he could not provide. It is clear that his request was public because the Healer both marveled and commented on it to those who followed Him. This centurion humbled himself to ask for help when he needed it, he approached Jesus, and he pleaded with Him. He is a good model for us.

Early College Experience

The earliest memory I have of asking for help was when I was in second grade. As I walked home from school in Cedarville, Ohio, I stopped by what is now Harriman Hall off the campus of Cedarville University. It is a large white house on the corner of Main and Chillicothe Streets. It was even larger in the eyes of that seven-year old boy.

College girls were holding a Bible club, which I attended on Thursday afternoons. On an afternoon in November 1955, just a month after my father and oldest brother had been hospitalized with polio, I followed my routine. There was a special speaker that day.

She was a very short woman who was a missionary in Africa in a country I have forgotten. She told a flannel graph story that I don't remember. She taught us a chorus in Swahili that I have also forgotten. But I remember her quoting John 3:16 over and over: "For God so loved the world, that he gave his only begotten Son, that whosoever believeth in him should not perish, but have everlasting life." She pointed her little, stubby finger at me, it seemed, every time she said "whosoever." I decided that day to ask for the eternal help I needed, and I asked Christ to be my Savior right there.

Harriman Hall became a dormitory for college students, and one of my children lived there as a university student years later. It was my first "college experience," and was both memorable and important. It was the place where I asked for—and received—the ultimate in help.

A Four-Star Button

I had several assignment locations as a captain, and one was at the Pentagon. I worked on the staff of the Secretary of the Air Force doing legislative liaison work. Most of my time that year, I provided information requested by members or staff from the House of Representatives and the Senate. It was fascinating and important work.

On occasion, I also escorted senior officers, including generals, to Capitol Hill for hearings or meetings with legislatiors. One morning I escorted a four-star general to the House Armed Service Committee for a public hearing that pertained to his area of responsibility.

He was sequestered in the Pentagon in an office for visiting generals preparing for the testimony he was about to give. I had arranged our car for the last leg of his trip, as he was using every available minute to prepare his testimony. At precisely the right minute when the car was standing by and we needed to depart, I knocked on the door and told him it was time to go. He stood and began buttoning his service dress suit coat. As he put the fourth button in place, it came off in his hand.

We both just stared at the button. Then he looked at me.

He didn't mouth any words for help, but his eyes shouted them. I stood there in front of his desk speechless. I was wearing a civilian suit I had just retrieved from the cleaners. I had removed the paper tag and slipped the attaching safety pin into my pocket. (My father grew up during the Depression Era, and I learned early not to throw good things away.) I unconsciously put my hand into my pocket and pulled out that safety pin. I stared at it as the general had stared at his button.

The rest was easy. This very junior officer and that very senior officer fumbled around with four hands and that tiny safety pin until we safely secured the button that everyone would see on the front of his coat as he testified before Congress.

It never hurts to ask for help when you need it. The failures that result from insufficient help can sometimes mark you for life. Asking for help only extends the group of people with whom you can share credit for the successes they'll help you lead.

I have found that writing things down, including those things with which I need help, is a good way to keep track of my intentions, goals, and tasks. For me, it is part of staying organized, and keeping a short list is part of this process.

Discussion Questions

1. Have you ever asked for help when you really didn't want to? How did it work out for the situation and for you?

2. What is the effect on an organization if a person asks for help more often than they need it? What is the effect on the individual doing the asking?

3. Whom do you know that is meek but not weak? What do they do or what have they done that demonstrates this?

4. What can a leader do in responding to someone who

asks for help that will throw open the door for others to ask when they are in need? Have you seen someone do this well or not well? What was the outcome?

5. Jacob and the centurion both humbled themselves in asking for help. For modern day leaders, would such an action impact their leadership? Why do you think so? Do you know any examples of leaders who have done this? What was the outcome?

Six

KEEP A SHORT LIST

There is more to keeping a short list than meets the eye. In addition to just keeping the list, there are the matters of keeping it short and what to put on it. All of these are important for leaders.

Keep a List

This is simple and important at the same time. I keep a list of things to do so I won't forget. Some things are so big, pressing, or visible they won't be forgotten. Others are in the gray area of probability of being remembered. Still others are good ideas or intentions but fall well below the threshold of recall in that they are context-related and are unlikely to re-present absent that context.

I have found that the discipline of writing it down, no matter the category, ensures it is there for consideration at the right time. A single process for all is more effective than multiple processes.

The only exception to putting something on a list is if I can "do it now." I saw the letters "DIN" engraved onto a brass plate, mounted on a nice wooden plaque, and placed above the desk of one of my bosses some years ago. Every time I went to his office, the plaque stared at me, and I didn't know what it meant. One day, I asked him, and he told me: "do it now."

It explained why he and others I had worked for did something I found peculiar at the time but which I later copied. If they took a phone call in the middle of a meeting with me, they would ask me to give them just another moment at the end of the call. They would then either make another phone call and assign an action or make a note of what they had just been discussing before proceeding with our conversation. They either "did it now" or they put it on a list.

Lists can be on paper or electronic aids, but they do need to be written down. Mental lists are more vulnerable to loss than visible, prominent, tangible, physical ones. I have learned several memory techniques that are effective for short-term recall, but they are more suited to public speaking or singular use. For example, it could be a grocery list, or it could be things taken away from or to be shared at a meeting.

Some people become disciplined at putting everything they are going to do on a list so they can check it off when they finished the task, or sometimes they put an "X" in a box by the item. I know people who get such satisfaction in X'ing boxes that they will write something they did that wasn't on the list, just so they can mark it off. I have been known to do that on occasion.

Some people have more than one list. I keep a running list of things I intend to complete "today or tomorrow." If I anticipate it will be longer, or if it has been hanging around for a couple of days, I put it on a mid-term list. Some things I don't intend to get to for some weeks or months, but they are still good ideas and intentions, so I put them on a longer-term list.

Keeping a list is the means; keeping it short is the end.

Keep it Short

The ultimate purpose in keeping a list is to accomplish the things you intend to do. Being disciplined to write things on a list but never completing them misses the point. The point is to write things down so that you will work them off. Keep the list short.

To be sure, some of yesterday's ideas and intentions won't seem as "bright" today, and you will change your mind about doing them. Mark it off. Other ideas will grow into larger ones or become part of other ideas. No problem. Mark it off. Some will be less urgent today than they were when you wrote them down; move it to a list with less urgency. Regardless of inevitable change, keep working the list down.

An even more important aspect of "keeping it short" deals with relationships. Issues in this area should be of the DIN-variety and not on a list. There will be times when a leader misspeaks or misunderstands. Sometimes he will offend or will be offended. Leaders will unintentionally make mistakes that can be either acts of commission or omission. All of these can damage relationships that can in turn reduce effectiveness and efficiency in an organization.

Deal with them right away—DIN! In these areas and ones like them, keep a *very* short list. Go out of your way to mend the fence, pick up the trash, right the wrong if possible, or apply healing salve if it is not. Relationships are enduring (as well as endearing), and keeping them strong is critical to present and future successes. They are the currency of necessary leadership transactions.

Finish by Sundown

Some years ago, my three-star boss took this lieutenant colonel with him to see the Air Force chief of staff. Not surprisingly, the other two did most of the talking. My boss looked to me a couple of times for responses to detailed questions, and, thankfully, I had the right answers. At the end of the meeting, the chief asked for some specific information. I'll never forget that he said, "I'd like to have it by sundown." We complied.

I had read the idea of "sundown" before. It was in Ephesians 4:26, in relation to strong feelings: "Be ye angry, and sin not: let not the sun go down upon your wrath."

Clearly, the Apostle Paul is saying it is okay to be angry but not to the point of sinning. Then he gives the sundown suspense on our wrath: get over it, and don't let it continue into the night or the next day. It is not coincidental that the very next verse continues the thought: "Neither give place to the devil."

When you notice the connecting punctuation between verses 26 and 27, it is clear that the former can lead to the latter if allowed to continue. Sunsets can be beautiful and peaceful when we release the anxieties of the day, or they can be stormy and weighty when we hang on to what we should release. The former is better.

Keeping Promises

Keeping promises is part of keeping short lists. The older I have gotten, the more careful I am in giving my word. Making one's word one's bond is a good way to live. As a leader, I learned quickly who exaggerated and who was more precise, who speculated and who knew, who promised and who delivered. Decisions leaders make are based on what subordinates say and promise. I came to value those who under-promised and over-delivered. I saw the same in what my bosses expected from me and my peers.

The day I was writing this in 2013, I received an e-mail from a friend who served with me a decade earlier. He updated me briefly on his family and job, about which he wrote, "When they hired me in June 2012, I told them I'd stay for at least two years, and I will live up to my word." It wasn't convenient for him, as he and his wife had moved a state away, but he took out a rental so he could keep his word. He commutes more than four hours home every other weekend. That is keeping a promise.

One senior Air Force officer I deeply respect and for whom I worked said on many occasions, "A promise made is a promise kept." He practiced this himself and expected it of his subordinates. It caused us to think carefully in making a promise and the commitment to follow through.

The ultimate promise-keeping example is the Lord. First Kings 8 tells a story about the wisest man ever:

> Solomon stood before the altar of the Lord in the presence of all the congregation of Israel, and spread forth his hands toward heaven. (vs. 22)

This isn't a private setting. Solomon, the king, is standing, not sitting, in plain sight of "all the congregation of Israel." If there was any doubt from his posture about whom he was addressing, it is cleared up in the next verse:

> And he said, Lord God of Israel, there is no God like thee, in heaven above, or on earth beneath. (vs. 23)

But the next part is the best. Solomon continues:

> Who keepest covenant and mercy with thy servants
> that walk before thee with all their heart. (vs. 23b)

This prayer is about God keeping His word. It is mentioned in the next three verses. But then after the lengthy prayer, Solomon summarizes it for us:

> And he stood, and blessed all the congregation of Israel
> with a loud voice, saying, Blessed be the Lord, that hath
> given rest unto his people Israel, according to all that
> he promised: there hath not failed one word of all his
> good promise, which he promised by the hand of
> Moses his servant. (vs. 55, 56)

Not one word of God had failed; He kept His promises. Leaders do the same, and they depend on those around them who do likewise.

Short List Items

Some notable leaders through the ages have kept a few items on their perpetual list of things to do. Daniel, whose leadership spanned from the Chaldean empire into the Persian one, had something on his "must-do" list: he would not defile himself.

> Daniel purposed in his heart that he would not defile
> himself with the portion of the king's meat, nor with
> the wine which he drank: therefore he requested of the
> prince of the eunuchs that he might not defile himself.
> (Daniel 1:8)

In the preceding verses, we see that Daniel's life had been turned upside down. He had been from Jerusalem about 800 miles to Babylon, and he didn't make the trip on an aircraft! His captors gave him a new education, language, and name, and they tried to give him a new god. There is no evidence that his family came with the young man, who was probably a teenager.

But despite all the disruption, Daniel had already put something on his list that he wouldn't let change—his purity before God. He wasn't going to "cave in" on this matter. He made the decision in his heart, and when confronted, he pushed back. When the first supervisor did not respond favorably to his request to avoid defiling himself, Daniel approached another. Note that he pushed back here but not in chapter 6, when his life was on the line.

While a leader might be willing to negotiate on some things, he should have a short list from which he is unwilling to deviate. He won't negotiate. He will push back. He will re-attack if necessary. Daniel had purity and regular prayer on his list. If a leader makes the "unwilling" list early, when an occasion presents itself there will be no uncertainty in the present or regret in the future.

Relationships

Even in the New Testament, keeping a short list plays out. Would it surprise you if I said the short list is tied to one of the ordinances of the church—communion? If this is the case, that would make it important.

First Corinthians 11 illustrates this. The order of the communion service, sometimes called "the Lord's supper," is outlined in verses 23 through 26. After a precaution about partaking "unworthily," this instruction is given:

> But let a man examine himself, and so let him eat of that bread, and drink of that cup. For he that eateth and drinketh unworthily, eateth and drinketh damnation to himself, not discerning the Lord's body. For this

cause many are weak and sickly among you, and many sleep.

Before partaking of the elements of the Lord's Supper, we are to examine ourselves and take care of things that would cause us to eat and drink unworthily. And you see the serious consequences if we don't. We need especially to make and keep our relationships right. If this short list is tied to communion, which it is, that should get our attention. Leaders keep this list very short, or better yet, at zero.

Relationships with others also deserve comment here. Matthew 7:3 states:

> And why beholdest thou the mote that is in thy brother's eye and not the beam that is in thine own eye?

Think of a mote as a splinter, and visualize a beam as a two-by-four or larger plank of wood. Jesus is using hyperbole here to ask why we see the minor mistakes of others without dealing with our own obvious faults and wrongdoings. Leaders give high priority to fixing relationship problems and keep the list of them short.

Can We Keep Him?

When we brought our youngest of three children home from the hospital, his older brother had just turned three. We had a special family time on the couch in our front room, and it was the first opportunity for our five-and-a-half-year-old daughter and younger son to hold the new baby.

We huddled and cuddled, and we talked and prayed. It was a very special time. I affirmed my wife but did the same for the two older children, knowing they needed attention because the newborn would be receiving a lot in the hours and days to come.

The children were attentive and thoughtful. I felt as though they received well all that I was trying to accomplish. I did note that the three-year-old was patiently waiting for a break in all I was saying so he could say something as I concluded our special time.

I asked him if he had anything he wanted to say. As only a three-year-old can do, he said, "Can we keep him?"

He had a short list, and keeping his new brother was at the top. He just had to know if he was going to be able to keep him.

Good Ideas

I have known junior and senior leaders who are idea generators. In a short conversation or meeting, they can generate a dozen or more ideas. They have astute minds and the ability to dream out loud. Some of their ideas are worthy, others less so. But they are prolific.

I have also observed that having some of these people around is useful. But more important than just having the ideas is accomplishing them.

This chapter has been about keeping a short list. While we need idea-generators, we also need list makers and list doers. Leaders who have fewer good ideas but who are also disciplined to keep a list and to keep it short get more done sometimes than the dreamers. I'm not saying that dreamers are undisciplined; but there is a different and necessary discipline to keeping a list and keeping it short.

Clearly this requires a degree of discipline. Another discipline is reading, and I have found that good leaders read to lead.

Discussion Questions

1. What are the pros and cons of keeping lists on paper and electronically? Which do you do, and what has been the effectiveness?

2. How would you decide whether to "do it now" or to put it on a list? What consideration do you give to the commitments you have made, to the expectations of others, and to expediency?

3. Recall an instance where you restored a bruised or broken relationship quickly or untimely. Why did you delay or decide not to delay? What was the outcome?

4. Do you know someone who kept a promise that hurt him or her? What did that look like, and what was the impact on his or her ability to lead?

5. What items are on the short list of things from which you won't back away? Have you or someone you know compromised on this, and if so, what was the result?

SEVEN

READ TO LEAD

"NO, NO... I HAVEN'T READ THEM. IT'S WALLPAPER."

Books may be one of the most underused resources available for leaders. Maybe it is because leaders are better at going than slowing, at rushing than reflecting, at pressing than resting. To sit and read requires putting the brain into a different gear.

I'm not talking about speeding through unread e-mails, the online news and sports, Early Bird news summaries, or a journal, though all those have their place. I am talking about sitting in the quiet and submerging up to your waist or even chest in a book you can't read in an hour.

We Don't Know Everything

Reading can obviously be an excellent source of information. So why is it that the higher up the leadership ladder we progress, the less reading we do? Having served in some big jobs, I can say it is not because senior leaders have all the answers. It seemed to me that the higher I went, the broader my responsibilities became and the more information I needed to just keep up.

When I was a senior Air Force officer, I periodically received books that were on a selected reading list. This made it convenient for me to stay current with what my peers were reading, and it continued to develop me in areas that benefitted me as a military leader. Some were historical or inspirational; others dealt with policy or strategy. All of them greatly helped me.

I have attended conferences where every attendee received a book. Given the cumulative expense, this is usually an indication that someone, probably the leader, thought this was a good selection for us.

I get ideas for good reading from other places. I sometimes buy books on reading lists from sources I respect. I am also always on the lookout for new books from some of my favorite authors: John Maxwell, Max Lucado, David Jeremiah, Mark Hitchcock, Clive Cussler, Jerry Jenkins, and other prolific and proven authors. Naming these authors gives away some of my interests, but it also reveals a way to limit the field of the thousands of books that become available each month. Balance is the key: new and proven authors, variety in subject matter, and reading that is wholesome.

Usually I have a stack of yet-to-be-read books waiting their turn, and sometimes others cut in line. You may also think there is no way to read the books people give and recommend to you, or those you obtain from other sources. That's fine; keep at it anyway, because good leaders are good readers.

There is value and enjoyment that come with reading. The value is in learning, and the enjoyment is in going places in your mind that you may not yet be able to visit in person.

New Ideas, Old Successes

Part of the value in reading goes beyond gaining information for today; it is also gathering ideas for tomorrow. I have told many young Air Force officers and college students that they need to read more than technical journals and material that is about their work.

When we read widely, we accumulate new ideas and learn about past successes. We shouldn't undervalue what has been accomplished before our time. Solomon, the wisest man ever, may have written the book of Ecclesiastes, in which he reminds us:

> There is no new thing under the sun. Is there any thing wherof it may be said, "See, this is new?" it hath been already of old time, which was before us. (1:10)

This is probably among the ten best-known passages from the Bible: "There is nothing new under the sun." People quote it without knowing it is Scripture. But it is Scripture and so true. So much written in the past merits the thoughtful leader's attention. Someone said, "It is better to learn from another's mistakes than from one's own." I won't argue with that.

Beyond learning the facts, history, personalities, successes, and failures of the past, good reading can fill us with hope, inspiration, and ideas for the present and future. New circumstances may not be all that new if we strip them down to their essence. The Ecclesiastes quote bears this out. In the last chapter, we covered asking for help when you need it. Now I'm suggesting that you do need help, and books are a great source of it.

Bring the Books

At the end of the Apostle Paul's life, he wrote to the younger Timothy. Sandwiched between two lists of names in 2 Timothy, Paul wrote, "bring…the books" (4:13).

Here is a man in the waning days of his life. The candle is about out of wax. The hourglass is running out of sand. The sun has set and darkness is coming. It is his last letter that we know of. Why in the world would he want "the books"?

Good leaders are good readers, we should read to lead, and we need to get into some books.

Read

It is a bit of a stretch to attach 1 Timothy 4:13 to the general topic of reading: "Till I come, give attendance to reading, to exhortation, to doctrine." I call it a stretch because the context of the passage is living, reading, preaching, meditating on, and obeying the Word of God. So I am not necessarily applying it to reading in general. But at the least, it is instruction to make reading Scripture part of our reading regimen, and to neglect it is to our own peril. At the most, it affirms reading in general. It is not a stretch, however, to see the importance of reading described in other passages:

> For whatsoever things were written aforetime were written for our learning, that we through patience and comfort of the Scriptures might have hope. (Romans 15:4)

> Thy Word is a lamp unto my feet, and a light unto my path. (Psalm 119:105)

It is the glory of God to conceal a thing: but the honour of kings is to search out a matter. (Proverbs 25:2)

Reading what others have written brings learning and insight for living, and when done with diligence, also brings honor.

A Memorial

The arguably greatest character in the Old Testament, Moses, didn't fight a battle recounted in Exodus 17. It occurs right after he smote the rock to provide water for the children of Israel, perhaps two million of them.

Then came Amalek, and fought with Israel in Rephidim. (vs. 8)

Moses instructed Joshua, his aide-de-camp, to lead the battle, while he took Aaron and Hur to the top of an overlooking hill.

And it came to pass, when Moses held up his hand, that Israel prevailed: and when he let down his hand, Amalek prevailed. (vs. 11)

As the battle raged below, Moses' arms got tired, so Aaron and Hur "stayed" them in the up position, and the Joshua-led Israelite army prevailed at the end of the day.

So what does this have to do with books and reading?

And the LORD said unto Moses, "Write this for a memorial in a book, and rehearse it in the ears of Joshua: for I will utterly put out the remembrance of Amalek from under heaven." (vs. 14)

The Lord knew His succession plan, and that it would be Joshua, many years later, who would be leading the Israelite army against the likes of Jericho and others. He also wanted him to remember well what had happened on an unknown plain below an unnamed hill.

In the Air Force, we often wrote after-action reports and lessons learned after significant events, but we read them less often. The result of not reading and heeding the lessons of the past was to "learn" them again and again. I suspect the same is true in other circles. There is much to read that can help us with today and tomorrow, and Moses made sure Joshua understood that.

Books and Others

The student of the Word will recall the role reading and books played in the lives of Daniel, Joshua, Samuel, Josiah, and Mordecai. Someone counted the number of references in the Bible to the words *records*, *chronicles*, and *book*. It numbers 192! The serious leader will consider bumping up their priority for reading, knowing that good leaders are good readers.

Reading from Afar

In the fall and winter of 1986–1987, my squadron took a rotation (we would call it a deployment today) to the United Kingdom. We were a C-130 squadron and would be gone between 60 and 90 days, flying resupply missions out of the United Kingdom to locations in Europe and around the Mediterranean Sea. There were a lot of positive things about the rotation. I was going to be flying in Europe (I was a navigator), experiencing other languages and cultures, growing the already warm camaraderie we had in the squadron, and encouraging the younger navigators, crewmembers, and maintainers.

I wasn't looking forward to being away from my family.

Those who have served in the military and have had to be away from family and home understand this conflicted view. With a loving and supportive wife and three young children aged eight, six, and three at our base in Texas, it was going to be family-difficult on both sides of the Atlantic.

Now this was "back in the day" before the technologies of Skype, e-mail, Internet, and cell phones. I decided to buy three children's Bible-story books, one for each of our kids, and to record the story for them using a cassette recorder. I figured if they were able to hear my voice whenever they wanted to, even in the context of reading a book, it would remind them of my love. I rang a little hand bell at the end of each page. Even our three-year-old figured out that if he turned the page when he heard the bell, he could see and hear the entire story from his dad without interruption.

They understood that I was far away, but in a way it brought me closer to them. This low-tech story reading helped encourage our children in my absence, but it also affirmed the value of reading at an early age.

What Are You Reading?

When I was a colonel and became a brigadier general around the year 2000, I was the advisor for the career broadening officers (CBOs) at the Oklahoma City Air Logistics Center (ALC) at Tinker Air Force Base. I took the advisor job seriously and became a mentor to these young officers, most of them captains.

The CBOs had come to the ALC on a special three-year assignment to broaden their respective careers. Most of them were aircraft maintenance officers who had distinguished themselves on the operational flight lines around the world. Each year, a special selection board met to consider which few should be moved into this program, which had benefits for the officer and the Air Force. They were outstanding officers with excellent records of performance. Each had significant potential.

I met with this group of six to ten officers on a recurring basis. We would sometimes meet for a brown bag lunch. Those times were more meeting than lunching. They knew I would quiz and challenge them. One question I would frequently ask was, "What are you reading that has nothing to do with your job?" Many were often working on advanced degrees at the time, so there was required reading for that. They were expected to keep up on professional journals and books too. But I pushed them to read broadly for their pleasure, development, and inspiration. More than once, the peer pressure kept a CBO from saying he or she wasn't reading anything.

Read in an Hour

Over the years, I have learned that all books aren't created equal. I read some books for pleasure, and read every word in every paragraph on every page. Other books are packed with historical or technical information, and I scan them until I find an area of interest and then slow down. Still others I read very quickly, including topical books where I try to get 80 percent of the information in 20 percent of the time it would otherwise take to read closely. I discuss this with the classes I teach because I think it has value to aspiring leaders.

A friend told me the title and cover of a book may be its two most important parts. I expect that is worthy of consideration for an author, but it also has value to a reader. I like to spend a little time where the author may have spent a lot. It gives me insight into the message of the book.

A second place where I pause is with the table of contents. It gives me clues to where I may want to spend more or less time reading. It also helps me grasp the author's organization of the book.

I also spend time reading the introduction closely. I have

found that a well-written introduction sometimes serves as a good summary of the entire book. Having read the table of contents and then the introduction, I already have a good handle on what the book is about.

When I turn the page into the first and subsequent chapters, I still look for clues. The chapter title and subtitles provide insight into key parts of the chapter. The first sentence in a paragraph is usually the topic sentence, and reading it alone facilitates speed. I linger with some paragraphs but move along with others. The hardest part is not going slow when I don't need to and accelerating when I can.

Using these techniques has helped me to read a book in an hour. I have found that comprehension is good and so is the amount of information I take from the book.

Any Suggestions?

Variety in reading is important. So here is a short list of a various genres of books that I have found inspirational.

Candice Millard wrote *The River of Doubt: Theodore Roosevelt's Darkest Journey.* It's a story of hope, despair, and of a great Brazilian explorer, Cândido Mariano da Silva Rondon. (My wife and I "read" this while listening to it on a CD while we drove cross county.)

David McCollough wrote *1776*, which details the military events of that year. Beyond recounting the start of our War for Independence, it gives insight into the relationship General George Washington had with the Continental Congress.

Tony Dungy's *Quiet Strength* is the story of the former National Football League Super Bowl-winning coach and the agony and ecstasy of his life. His inner Strength was his quiet strength.

Disciplines of a Godly Man by R. Kent Hughes is as useful, timely, direct, and challenging a book as a young or older man would want to read. The title describes exactly what it is about.

Bruce Olson's *Bruchko* is the story of a very young man who lived through significant hardship and changed an institution.

The Bible. No list of good, inspirational books would be complete without the Bible.

In this short list of books you see history, strong characters, a president, a general, a coach, sports, death, adventure, discipline, and a thousand dangers, successes, and ideas. The inspiration abounds.

But as I read books like these, I look for things I can also apply to the leadership position I am in at the time. Millard's book encouraged me to endure hardship, McCollough's to communicate up the chain, Dungy's to give family high priority, Hughes's to keep godliness the highest priority, and Olson's to go bravely where others haven't trod. I look beyond inspiration in general to encouragement in particular.

I talked about writing this book for a long time. When I struggled with how to get started, my wife said, "Just start writing." The same is true about reading to lead: just start reading.

In your reading, you'll see how leaders have handled success and failure. Both result from how well they set the course and pace.

Discussion Questions

1. What are the excuses we use to justify not having time to read? Why is each not valid?
2. Are there valid reasons for not reading? Which, if any, is long-term?
3. What have you read recently that is not directly related to your job or studies? What kind of books would you read if you were to read more?
4. Which is better: inspired or assigned reading? Why? How would you get peers and subordinates in your

vocation to read more and to read more beneficially?

5. What benefit does writing have for the leader? Which is more valuable to the leader: reading or writing?

6. What are the merits and pitfalls of reading lists?

EIGHT

SET THE COURSE ...
AND THE PACE

On a mission, flight or otherwise, leadership sets the course and the pace. Many people have written of the former, few of the latter. To "set the course" is to lead, the conventional wisdom goes. Consider the emphasis placed on setting the vision; to mission, goals, and objectives; and to getting a job done. If we don't know where we are going, how can we get there? "A failure to plan is a plan for failure." "It's better to aim at something and miss it than to aim at nothing and hit it." You've heard all these clichés and more.

Set the Course

Let me be clear, setting the course is important. A leader who fails to set the course doesn't take the organization, family, team, unit, or company forward. There may well be movement—words like *flounder*, *thrash*, and *wasted energy* come to mind—but there won't be purposeful movement toward a predetermined objective. We need managers to manage processes, but leaders have to take people forward or they aren't leading.

Leaders must set the Proverbs' vision: "Where there is no vision, the people perish" (29:18). Leaders seldom inherit a vision. That is part of why we need them—to think big, to marshal resources, to inspire subordinates. This is true in military endeavors and civilian ones alike. Recall the boldness and complexity of General Eisenhower's planning for the invasion at Normandy on June 6, 1944. Or President Kennedy's challenge to put a man on the moon "before the decade is out," a challenge that was met in July 1969.

There are many other examples of vision that are worthy of consideration: Lt. Col. Jimmy Doolittle's launch off the deck of the USS Hornet in April 1942, Ernest Shackleton's explorations of Antarctica in the early 1900s, the Lewis and Clark expedition a century earlier, and General George Washington's Christmas Eve raid across the Delaware River in 1776.

All these exemplified various aspects of setting the course. Eisenhower saw as possible what others couldn't imagine. Kennedy challenged science to push the learning curve. Doolittle saw potential in B-25 bombers and an aircraft carrier that others didn't. Shackleton accurately stated the enormity of the challenge and yet still attracted men hardy enough to beat the odds. Lewis and Clark responded to a president's challenge and brought their respective strengths to bear on obstacles they couldn't have foreseen. Washington seized opportunity by winning a rare victory that had strategic implications.

As important as it is to set the course, effective leaders also have to set the pace. This requires moral courage.

...and the Pace

There will be times when a leader has to get followers to move faster than they are comfortable moving. This isn't popular, but then popularity isn't the number one goal of a leader. It shouldn't even be in a leader's top ten goals! Subordinate leaders with a clear view of the senior leader's vision will have a good feel for the necessary pace, that is, the speed at which things need to move along to accomplish tasks and arrive at the goal. Moving faster takes moral courage, but so does slowing things down.

Going slower can be harder than going faster. I have observed it is a greater challenge to go slower in order to reduce or mitigate risk, eliminate safety concerns, or to care for personnel (not personal) needs. Leaders of smaller undertakings or organizations win favor and often get promoted on the basis of their successful performance at that level. They aren't promoted based on performance but on potential. And what is the best indication of potential? Performance.

So there is a natural reluctance to ask for more time, thus my "moral courage" assessment. Though usually unfounded, subordinates sometimes think their seniors will disparage them if they don't "deliver" on time, every time.

I have observed that senior leaders are very understanding when a subordinate asks for more time and lays out the logic clearly. I have also observed that subordinate leaders who always have a "reason" for not delivering on time have either a planning or execution deficiency that can lead to being marginalized, replaced, or moved as a leader.

Slowing things down on occasion is necessary. If it becomes the practice, however, it is usually because there are either unrealistic expectations or promises, neither of which reflects well on the respective leader.

Come Over and Help Us

Early in the book of Acts, we see the Apostle Paul as an official of the established religion, a leader in his own right, who went about persecuting the new church of believers in Christ. Following his conversion to faith in Christ on the road to Damascus, his life changed.

There are a couple of times in Paul's life when he demonstrated the principle of setting the course and pace. The first was early in his post-conversion ministry, and the second was at the end.

In Acts 16:7-12, we read:

> After they were come to Mysia, they assayed to go into Bithynia: but the Spirit suffered them not. And passing by Mysia came down to Troas. And a vision appeared to Paul in the night; there stood a man of Macedonia, and prayed him, saying "Come over into Macedonia, and help us." And after he had seen the vision, immediately we endeavored to go into Macedonia, assuredly gathering that the Lord had called us for to preach the gospel unto them. Therefore loosing from Troas, we came with a straight course to Samothracia, and the next day to Neapolis. And from thence to Philippi, which is the chief city of that part of Macedonia and a colony: and we were in that city abiding certain days.

This passage contains three references to setting the course and pace. Verse 10 says Paul responded "immediately." Given that he had seen the vision in the night (verse 9), there is nothing to indicate he even waited until the normal rising time the next morning. It says "immediately." He had "assuredly gathered that the Lord had called" his companions and him to go into Macedonia, and he got right after it. He set out immediately. That is setting the pace. He had orders "from headquarters," so to speak, and he moved out.

The second reference to our maneuver is in verse 11. Luke, the author of Acts, says, "We came with a straight course" to Samothracia. They didn't divert into Athens for supplies. They didn't delay for a recommendation from the council in Jerusalem. They went around the north end of the Aegean Sea right into Macedonia and two of its cities, first Neapolis, and then Philippi. They moved out and on a "straight course."

The third reference is at the end of the passage where Luke writes, "and we were in (Philippi) abiding certain days." I see in this concluding comment both elements of this principle. They had reached their objective (the course), and they stayed there for a period of time (the pace).

A Good Fight

This trip to Macedonia was on Paul's second of three missionary journeys and before the trip to Rome at the end of his life. While in Rome, at the end, he wrote his letter to his younger protégé, Timothy:

> For I am now ready to be offered, and the time of my departure is at hand. I have fought a good fight, I have finished my course, I have kept the faith: Henceforth there is laid up for me a crown of righteousness, which the Lord, the righteous judge, shall give me at that day:

and not to me only, but unto all them also that love his appearing. (2 Timothy 4:6–8)

We see both elements of the maneuver in this passage, especially in verse 7. Paul writes that he has "fought a good fight." If you have ever watched fighters enter a boxing ring, each spends some time measuring his opponent. This isn't a frenetic phase of the fight. What follows is an all-out effort combined with more time of measuring and deflecting the blows throughout the fight.

It is like this in life, ministry, service, work, and about anything we do. At the start, there is a time for learning, then activity, perhaps even aggressiveness, then assessing with appropriate action throughout. Paul summarized his life by saying he had "fought a good fight." He had set and kept a good pace.

I have known leaders who start out well but do not finish well. Others start slowly and finish strongly. Even better are those who start well and finish well. Though life is a marathon, not a sprint, there are times when we have to sprint. It is all-important to set the pace.

In verse 7 Paul also wrote, "I have finished my course." It is clear that he had a course he was tracking, and he finished what he started. He didn't stop part way or leave it to others to do. He finished it all. He had a course, he tracked to it, and he finished it.

Finally, note the conclusion of verse 7: "I have kept the faith." While he was pacing himself and tracking along the course, he didn't lose sight of the most important part of the journey—his faith, from which he never diverted his attention.

Brisbane to Guam

When I was a young navigator on the C-130E, a medium-sized cargo aircraft, our crew had brought some necessary cargo to

Royal Australian Air Force Base Amberley. We were to return to the US territory of Guam a couple of days later. The flight to Guam was about 3,000 miles to the north given our route of flight, and the flying time would be about ten hours. Quite obviously, we were flying from a large, known location to a small island a long way away.

This story shows the importance of flying a straight course. At our airspeed of nearly 300 knots, missing our desired course by just a single degree would produce a 5-mile error of position in an hour and a 50-mile cumulative error over the ten-hour flight. Before the exquisite electronic equipment modern-day airliners enjoy, 1950s technology with which our plane was equipped made such precision difficult. If we erred by an average of 4 degrees, we would miss Guam by 200 miles and neither see it on radar nor lock on to its radio navigation aids.

We departed with all our navigation aids operating properly. I had preflight-checked them, and all seemed well. While this 1976 flight was before either inertial navigation systems or global positioning systems, we had no shortage of equipment to assist the navigator on such transoceanic flights. But bad things began to happen. No single problem would have been catastrophic, but the cumulative effect of many failures was, as we say, "of concern."

The radar was useful for portraying land-water contrast, but the absence of land or islands on this flight rendered it useless as a navigational aid.

The sextant was a magnificent piece of equipment, and I was skilled in using it to find lines of position from sighting the sun, moon, and even planets during day and stars by night. But the port in the top of the aircraft froze up, and we could not extend the periscopic sextant to a position where I could use it. So it too became useless.

The Doppler was excellent at displaying drift angle and

ground speed over land and even over water if the waves were rough enough to return our signals for interpretation. But the sea was so calm that we couldn't get a signal in the smooth sea mode.

The radio altimeter, with careful readings and accurate mathematical calculations, could show the drift angle and help assign a proper heading, or course. Its biggest limitation was that this process didn't work within 20 degrees of the equator given the minimal changes in barometric pressure. We traversed the equator and thus were within 20 degrees for most of the flight.

Our aircraft was equipped with an early version of long-range air navigation equipment that was useful for finding lines of position. It worked well over water, but that day it wasn't providing any useful information in the part of the Pacific over which we were flying.

We were also equipped with the dependable and accurate VHF omnidirectional range and tactical air navigation systems. Unfortunately, the systems only work about 200 miles from the ground stations, and in the absence of islands and land stations, we could use neither after the first hour of flight.

But we also had automatic direction finding equipment that sensed signals from ground-based nondirectional beacons that could have guided us in to Guam. Unfortunately, for reasons I don't recall, that was not an option the day we were flying.

We had two compass systems. One of them failed, and the other was unreliable.

The autopilot was tied to one of the compass systems, so the pilot had to "hand-fly" the aircraft.

Finally, we had a standby compass. We called it a whiskey compass because the compass rose floated in alcohol instead of water, which would freeze at high altitudes. The fist-sized, free-floating compass was all we had, and the pilots, skilled as they were, had an enormous challenge to stay on the desired heading.

I did have one other aid to navigation. While we cruised at more than three miles above the ocean, I saw clouds below us that looked like the cornrows near my boyhood home in Cedarville, Ohio. It looked to me as though the wind was blowing the clouds from our back left to our front right, and I surmised we had about two degrees of right drift and about a ten-knot tail wind. With dead reckoning, I plotted our course, prayed a lot to the One who put the stars in place, even though I couldn't use them this day, and we flew northward.

When my computed position indicated we were 200 miles south of Guam, we declared an emergency due to minimal navigation aids, and asked for a vector to our base. There was a long silence. The air traffic controllers told us to fly our present heading and that we were within half a mile of course. What a relief.

You see, it was important that we set exactly the right course and that we set exactly the right pace.

Winchester

On another long Pacific Ocean flight that same year, my crew and I were flying from Kwajalein Atoll in the Marshall Islands to Hickam Air Force Base in Hawaii, an eight-hour flight, as I recall.

Our aircraft commander was one of the wisest and most accomplished pilots with whom I ever flew. Like me, the co-pilot was a young lieutenant. He also went on to a successful career in the Air Force. In fact, I worked for him 33 years later, and we both remember this story well.

As we flew northeast on our course toward Hawaii, we were comfortably at our altitude of about three miles high. Unlike what happened in the previous story, all our navigational aids were working fine, and I was quite busy doing the mathematical computations that converted mechanical and electrical signals and readings into lines of position (LOP). Crossing these LOPs marked our location and confirmed our dead reckoning position, that is, the spot I computed based on heading, expected wind vector, and airspeed. Everything looked good.

The rudimentary equipment on my aircraft helped me position it on a chart after near-constant calculations for 20 to 30 minutes at a time. A single error in the math would result in an inaccurate position. On the size chart we used, even the width of the pencil mark was more than five miles. We lacked the much newer equipment like the C-5 aircraft's inertial navigation system (INS), which provides accurate coordinates for immediate plotting with the push of a button.

While I worked away, the pilots saw contrails coming toward us, but it was quickly apparent that the aircraft leaving the vapor trail was well above us in altitude. As it came closer, it looked as though it would pass directly overhead in the opposite direction but along the same airway.

I don't remember if it was the pilot or co-pilot who first suggested that it might be a C-5 aircraft, a very large cargo-carrying aircraft from our command. Knowing that the crew might be monitoring on our radio frequency, we called them at a frequency of 303.0, nicknamed "Winchester" after the 30.30 rifle. We didn't know their call sign, so we called for any aircraft at our position. To my surprise (and delight), one responded.

Indeed, it was a C-5 that we knew had the consistently accurate dual INS coupled to the autopilot for hands-off and accurate positioning and flying. The plane was flying more than six miles above the water, so we couldn't see it very well, but its contrails made tracking it easy. We asked them to give us their INS coordinates on our mark, which we gave as they passed directly above us. At that moment, the plane was three miles directly above us.

It was the easiest position I ever plotted! It took me less than 30 seconds to write down the coordinates they gave us and to put them on the chart with the traditional small triangle navigators use to show their present position. Voila! The C-5's INS showed we were exactly where I thought we were, and we were on the centerline of our planned course.

That is a good place for a leader to be—on the centerline of the course he plans.

There is a post-script to this flight. The co-pilot of that flight wrote me a handwritten note that he gave me when I retired from the Air Force in 2012. I now treasure that letter, in which he wrote: "Dear Loren, our professional association and friendship goes back many years to your and Karen's taking care of the single guys, to ultra-precision on the aircraft, to extraordinary skills on the basketball court."

He remembered the Winchester assist that confirmed our course, and he went on to plot an ambitious and necessary course for our Air Force in very difficult times. Good leaders pursue precision in all they do. What a great leader he was— then and since.

New Commander's Guidance

When I was a young colonel, I had the privilege of commanding a large technical training group. Counting students, faculty, and staff, there were 5,200 military and civilian members for whom I was responsible. Ours was an important mission—training new airmen in the Air Force to lead and serve as comptrollers, crew chiefs, carpenters, electricians, plumbers, avionics technicians, communication system technicians, pneudraulic technicians, weapon loaders, maintenance officers, and more.

I remember the day I took command. What a glorious ceremony: watching the troops pass in review, taking the guidon of command (a flag on a staff that is unique to that particular unit), hearing my name announced as the new commander, listening to the band play the familiar marches, and meeting my subordinate commanders for the first time.

Another important part of the day was my briefing with my new boss. The two-star general was seasoned, experienced in both command and technical training, and well respected in the Air Training Command and Air Force hierarchies. I had a thirty-minute appointment with him, and I was fully ready to receive his commander's guidance. I expected a long list of things he wanted me to do, insight into his pet peeves, and an explanation of the things he wanted me to fix.

I reported in with a salute according to military custom. He received me warmly into his office. He asked how we had weathered the move, how my wife was doing, if our three children were settled into school (it was early September), and how our on-base house was. He was most cordial in those opening two minutes. Then he got down to business.

As best I can recall, he then said the following: "There are two things I'd like you to do. Get along with the other colonels, and let me know if something goes wrong before my boss calls me about it." I attentively wrote down exactly what he had said, told him I'd do it, and was ready for more. He stood and walked to the door. He extended his hand toward me. I rose, shook his hand, saluted, and departed. The meeting took all of three minutes. That was it. Get along, and keep him informed in a timely manner.

As I reflect on what he told me, I see he was setting the course and pace for me. To get along with my peers was the course he wanted me to take, and to keep him timely informed was the pace. He put the principle of this entire chapter in two brief phrases. Good leaders set the course and the pace. But as difficult as this is, showing accountability is perhaps even more difficult.

Discussion Questions

1. Recall a leader you know who did a good job setting the course. How did that person decide on the course and then communicate it to others?

2. When a leader is new to an organization, what sources should he or she consult in determining the course to set, and how long should he or she take?

3. Finish this sentence: A leader who doesn't show moral courage in setting the pace _____. Why do you think that?

4. Which is harder for a leader in setting the pace: to speed a team up or to slow it down? Have you or someone you know done either? What was the result over the short- and long-term?

5. At the end of Paul's life, he said, "I have finished my course." At the end of your life, what will be the items on your "course"?

6. When next you are the leader of a team, what "commander's guidance" will you give to newcomers? Is it important to reach out to newcomers? Why?

7. To what extent should leaders set the course and pace in their personal lives in addition to the organization's agenda? What are the biggest personal challenges for you?

NINE
SHOW ACCOUNTABILITY

"YEAH? WELL, "BEATS ME" HARDLY EXPLAINS THIS!"

L eadership requires a leader to show accountability. Without accountability, a leader loses effectiveness and credi-
bility with subordinates and the confidence of seniors.

Two Kinds of Accountability

When we talk about accountability, the first thing that comes to
mind is that someone has done something wrong, and the leader
needs to get to the bottom of it—now. Senior leaders investigate
to get to the bottom of the wrong. They ask probing questions
and search for the root cause. They sometimes take adverse personnel actions if merited. These may include verbal or written

counseling, admonishment, reprimand, retraining, replacement, or firing. In the military, the wrong deed could result in court-martial. I understand the difference between mistakes and crimes, and only the latter merits criminal action.

Someone caused this to happen, the leader is bent on finding out who and why, and on taking the appropriate action. The leader will hold people accountable.

These are the things that run through a leader's mind when something goes wrong. An effective leader, however, responds just as diligently when things go right.

If something has gone right, what action should the leader take? As with something that's gone wrong, it didn't happen by itself; someone was responsible and should be held accountable in a positive way.

As with the negative, there are also many ways to hold a person positively accountable for his or her actions. Leaders and supervisors can commend the person, recognize the right-doer in front of peers, write a letter of praise, or send the person's superiors a written account of the event. A leader can reward, award, or promote the person. The leader can take a picture, tell about the "incident" in a staff meeting, or put it in a company publication.

The effective leader is as tenacious about excellence as with failure. To be clear, not every success or failure requires the highest praise or most severe form of correction. The issue is balance. Effective leaders do both well and consistently. Responding proportionately to the failure or success is a leader's duty. The key is to praise *and* reprimand. The leader who praises often but corrects seldom will see discipline erode. The leader who corrects often and praises seldom will find people working in fear. Neither is healthy for an organization.

The other key is proportionality. If praise is over-the-top for a meager success, the leader won't have margin to appropriately reward or recognize a greater success. The inverse is true about dealing with failures. If a leader views every problem as a nail and every solution as a hammer, the leader loses the ability to tailor the response. *Proportionate* and *appropriate* are close relatives in this matter.

Show versus Require

The title of this chapter is "Show Accountability." I have talked about accountability to my military associations for years. For a long time, I talked about requiring accountability. Given the culture in the military as well as in civilian ventures, subordinates need to understand they will be held accountable.

In the Air force, this was important in the field of aircraft maintenance. Young airmen who are properly trained and experienced have the authority and trust to be the last one to sign off on a mechanical corrective repair to the aircraft before a flight. That is a great responsibility, but one I have seen them carry well. Accountability comes with that responsibility. They understand they will be held accountable for their actions, and they are diligent to be sure they do the repair or inspection right. The entire aircraft maintenance system relies on this trust and required accountability.

We all understand this aspect of accountability. Subordinates and superiors "get it." But another part of accountability is even more powerful.

Leaders must not only hold their subordinates accountable, they need to show it in themselves. I have not worked for a single leader who did not make a mistake or at least misspeak on occasion. Someone said the only person who doesn't make mistakes is the person who isn't doing anything.

When a leader makes a mistake, whether of omission or commission, he or she is faced with a dilemma: admit it and risk losing the confidence of superiors and subordinates alike, or mask it and hope no one will find out, thus keeping the reputation intact.

I have found this dilemma to be counterintuitive. While the leader thinks he or she risks losing confidence and esteem, it is just the opposite. Most of the time, subordinates and sometimes superiors already know, and the leader masks it to his own peril. Masking an error elevates it from an esteem issue to one of integrity. By admitting what others probably already know, the leader is seen as transparent, honest, and fair, increasing the esteem, trust, and confidence of subordinates. The leader brings into the open his own faults just as he does the faults of others.

The dilemma is also shortsighted. More often than not, even if no one else knows about the mistake, it will eventually come to light. When that happens, the result will be far more problematic than if it had been revealed up front. If a leader lets his integrity slip, the basis for his superiors' confidence also slips, and that is a precursor for moving on to a "new line of work!"

Accountability has both a negative and a positive side, and effective leaders require it of others and show it themselves.

Joshua Rises to the Occasion

One of my favorite characters in the Bible is Joshua—General Joshua—in the Old Testament. For 40 years, he was the aide-de-camp to Moses, the great patriarch. It is a fascinating study to see all the things he observed and did in this aide position, but that exceeds the scope of our study here.

Soon after Joshua took over from Moses, he led the children of Israel across the Jordan River and against the mighty walled city-state of Jericho. On the seventh day of the siege, the walls fell in on the city, and Israel marched in and conquered the bastion.

Joshua moved right on to the next city, Ai, which was much smaller and less protected than Jericho had been. Joshua sent "men" (we don't know how many) to spy out the adversary, and they returned with a report that was well received. They told Joshua:

> Let not all the people go up; but let about two or three thousand men go up and smite Ai; and make not all the people to labor thither; for they are but few. So there went up thither of the people about three thousand men: and they fled before the men of Ai. And the men of Ai smote of them about thirty and six men: for they chased them. (Joshua 7:3–5)

This didn't end well. They faced a much smaller adversary, sent an adequate force, and may even have had the element of surprise. But they were thrashed. In response, Joshua tore his clothes, fell to the earth, and put dust on his head. He asked God why. The root cause is stated in verse 1: "Achan…took the accursed thing, and the anger of the LORD was kindled against the children of Israel."

"The accursed thing" refers to booty that Achan had taken from Jericho, defying the Lord's command that everything in the city be destroyed. Because of this disobedience by one man, the whole nation suffered, and Israel failed against a lesser adversary. God told Joshua: "Thou canst not stand before thine enemies until ye take away the accursed thing from among you" (vs. 12).

Now it is time for Joshua, the leader, to hold Achan, the subordinate, accountable. God gave Joshua specific instructions about what to accomplish the next morning. Note Joshua's response. First, he "rose up early in the morning" (see verse 16). He didn't call a staff meeting, he didn't contemplate his actions through a hearty breakfast, and he didn't wait until the eleventh hour. No, he rose early. That is a good thing for leaders to do, especially when there is tough business to tend to.

After Joshua identified Achan as the culprit, Joshua said to him:

> Why hast thou troubled us? The Lord shall trouble thee this day. And all Israel stoned him with stones, and burned them [the accursed items, his children, and all his possessions] with fire after they had stoned them with stones. (vs. 25)

Note several things. First, Achan was held accountable. Subordinates need to understand that leaders will hold them accountable. Second, it was the Joshua's duty to hold one subordinate accountable, and he "rose up early in the morning" to take care of business. Third, unaccounted-for mistakes or errors can lead to serious consequences. In this case, it cost the lives of thirty-six men. Fourth, it had consequences for more than just Achan. It cost the lives of his children.

I will leave it to more wise theologians than me to explain two things. Were Achan's children included in the judgment because God intended to erase his lineage? And second, there is no mention of Mrs. Achan; perhaps the mercy of God spared her because she was not of Achan's bloodline.

What a horrible set of consequences due to the greed of a single person: defeat in battle, the death of soldiers, and the loss of a family. But the overarching principle is one of showing accountability. Joshua responded appropriately and in public to what had been done in secret.

Daniel: Guilty or Innocent?

Another biblical example, unlike the negative consequences for Achan, was quite positive. It is one of the best-known stories in the entire Bible, told in Daniel 6. The king had been tricked into signing a decree that forced him to command that Daniel be "cast into the den of lions.... And a stone was brought and laid upon the mouth of the den; and the king sealed it with his own signet and with the signet of his lords; that the purpose might not be changed concerning Daniel" (vs. 16–17).

It is not an attribute of wise leaders to "sign before reading" or to direct actions without understanding the consequences, which is what the king had done in this case. To his credit, however, he "arose very early in the morning and went in haste unto the den of lions" (vs. 19).

As Joshua did, the king attended to this injustice by rising "very early in the morning" and proceeding "in haste." What happens next is significant.

The king called to Daniel and asked if he had survived the night with the lions. I expect he waited to hear a voice, as I did approaching Guam after a long flight with no navigational aids— just hoping for a response. Daniel's response is instructive:

> O king, live for ever. My God hath sent his angel and hath shut the lions' mouths, that they have not hurt me; forasmuch as before Him innocence was found in me; and also before thee, O king, have I done no hurt. (vs. 21, 22)

We're talking about accountability. Daniel tells the king that he was spared the lions' mouths because he was found to be innocent. One cannot be found innocent if he is not examined. God examined Daniel and found him innocent. The king had condemned Daniel, but God found him innocent. I would rather it happen this way than for man to find me innocent and God to find me guilty. Daniel had his priorities right.

The last five words in verse 22, "Before thee, O king, have I done no hurt," are more than an add-on. Daniel told the king something about his response to what the king had done. Daniel had done no hurt to the king. He did not speak ill of the king. He did not harbor a grudge. He did not harm the king's reputation. "Before thee, O king, have I done no hurt." God held Daniel accountable, and then Daniel held himself accountable. To show accountability is to do what Daniel modeled.

Nine-Ship Airdrop

I alluded to this story earlier in the book, and it is useful here too. Having led a formation of eight aircraft around a low-level route, I proceeded down the wrong side of a drop zone, given the direction of the strong crosswind, and ordered the release of a load that came to rest far from its desired landing zone. My fellow crewmembers had tried to convince me I was reading the wind backwards, but I didn't listen. As I wrote earlier, "Predictably, my load landed well off the drop zone to the right, off the reservation, and was unrecoverable in the jungle." The results were more than embarrassing, but I owned them. It was entirely my fault.

Beyond shouldering the blame, however, there is a point about accountability in this story. When we landed back at the base, there were people waiting for me. They knew my strike report before I did. They had questions; I said, "Yes, sir." They talked. I listened. It was accountability.

Upon reaching the squadron, I "enjoyed" more of the same. There were more questions and more "yes, sirs." It was a very long afternoon. I was properly held accountable for my error in judgment. I learned a lot of things: depend on co-workers, don't shout them down, and expect that they might see something in a situation that has escaped my attention. I was ready to just go home and retreat into my cave.

My wife, Karen, met me at the door. She was so happy to see me and couldn't wait to introduce me to another squadron wife who was in our living room. Karen insisted I let her tell me what she had seen. I demurred. She insisted. I yielded only as my wife pulled me to the big living room chair, seated me, sat on my lap, and put her arms around my neck. She proceeded to tell the story of what she had seen.

"My husband was the number two in a large formation of C-130s, and all the others followed him instead of the 'bozo' in the lead aircraft whose load landed in the jungle. I am so proud of my husband and am certain that the navigator on the lead aircraft must be feeling really badly about now." She had no idea how badly!

I was held accountable for an unsatisfactory result to something over which I had complete control. I deserved all I received.

Some people have asked me about the consequences of this mistake. First, I suggest that a consideration of consequences should not prevent taking accountability. Second, though there were the near-term consequences of embarrassment, decertification, and retraining, my commander was wise and didn't treat it as a fatal flaw. Third, I certainly learned from the experience and used it to become a better navigator and leader. Fourth, as I progressed in my career, it reminded me that I am less than perfect and that others' flaws aren't necessarily fatal ones.

Commander's Coin

Many years later, I held a young airman accountable for something he did well, and the results reverberated across the miles.

Before I joined the Air Force in 1973, I taught school in Jamestown, Ohio. In my eighth-grade science class in my second year of teaching, I enjoyed the presence of a very good student named Debbie. As the years passed, she spied me out on the Internet and noted that I was still on active duty in the Air Force more than thirty-five years later.

After I retired, she asked if she and her husband could come to visit me when they came back to Ohio from Nebraska, where they now made their home. Delighted to hear from her after all those years, we set the day and time for her visit.

While we were visiting, she told me that several years earlier, her Air Force son was a security forces airman stationed at a base in the Republic of Korea. She sent him my biography from the Internet and asked if he had ever seen or heard of me.

He replied by e-mail that he not only had seen me, but I had given him one of my coins—a custom senior officers and NCOs use to recognize excellence right on the spot. I remembered the incident as she told me the story.

I was visiting his base and asked to be taken to the security forces posts for a no-notice check of these well-trained and hard-working young men and women who serve well out of the limelight so faithfully.

I remember approaching this impeccably groomed young airman who snapped to attention and offered me as crisp a salute as one could hope to receive. He then proceeded to give me a post briefing in which he explained the limits of his responsibility, chain of command, effective range of the weapons he was carrying, and everything else about his post that I asked of him. In short, he was superb in every aspect of what I heard and observed. So, I gave him one of my coins.

He had told his mother of the incident, and she reported it back to me, half a world away and several years later. I held him positively accountable for his excellence, and it reverberated through his squadron and wing, and then across the water to his mother's ears and to mine. This sometimes happens when we hold people positively accountable for their actions.

Handshake with a Sergeant's Son

I was stationed in the Pentagon in my last assignment, and encountered something I wanted to affirm. A young sergeant was out-processing on his way to a deployment to southwest

Asia, and he had brought his four-year-old son along. I thought it was noteworthy that a father would bring his young son with him as he tended to administrative necessities on his last day before going to a combat zone, and I wanted to encourage the dad.

I left my office a few minutes early on the way to a meeting. Walking into the outer office area, I saw the sergeant and his son. The sergeant was at a desk talking with an orderly taking care of some paperwork. The son was reclining on the couch with his feet up on the back, his head on an armrest, and his arms flung carelessly above his head. The father came to attention. The son did not.

The father showed frustration that his four-year-old son did not respond to the general as the father knew to. The looks from the father to the son spoke more volumes to me than to the son. The former was standing tall, and the latter was so very relaxed!

I intervened. I went right over to the son and began talking with him. He warmed up to me quickly. We chatted. I asked if he knew where his father was going. He said, "Yes, to the ice cream store on the way home." We both enjoyed the exchange. I barely noticed some moisture on the lad's right hand as I was weighing whether or not I had appeased the father's chagrin.

As the minutes passed, it came time for me to move along to my meeting down the hallway. Surmising that I had repaired the damage, I extended my right hand to the youngster wanting to shake his hand, encourage him, and depart.

With my hand extended for more than a few seconds, I observed that he was not reciprocating. Instead, he was wiping his hand on his shirt. I had no idea what he was doing, but wanting to identify with him, I did the same.

The young boy saw what I was doing and said, loud enough for his father and all in the office to hear, "So you still suck your thumb too?" If the father was chagrined before, he now was mortified. We all laughed, and I went on to my meeting.

I had tried to hold the father positively accountable for bringing his son along on such a special day, but it didn't work out the way I had intended. Holding people positively accountable won't always work out as we intend, but good leaders do it anyway. They are willing to take the chance.

Flat Tire

When I was a colonel stationed at Tinker Air Force Base in Oklahoma, I was invited to address a group in California on a Saturday. I don't remember if it was an Air Force Reserve Officer Training Corps or an Air Force Association audience. Regardless, I flew on a commercial jet to Los Angeles International Airport (LAX) in my short-sleeved uniform and didn't carry any luggage. The agenda took me out to LAX in the morning, to the venue to speak at noon, and back in the late afternoon.

Everything went as planned on the leg out, the drive to the speaking engagement, the speech, and the drive back toward LAX. But on the side of the freeway north of the airport, I saw a car pulled to the side with an obvious left front flat tire. Seeing a lady standing to the rear of the disabled car, I decided to circle around and offer assistance.

After the appropriate turns, exits, and reentering the freeway to approach from behind her, I pulled off and put on the rental car's flasher lights. I told the lady I had noticed her flat tire and offered to change it for her. She thanked me for responding so quickly. Surprised, I asked her what she meant. She "informed" me I was from the California Highway Patrol and she appreciated the quick response. I told her I was actually in the Air Force, but I had stopped to help her with her flat tire.

She "informed" me again that she didn't have a flat but rather she had blown her transmission. Her late model Mercedes Benz looked fine to me except for the flat tire. I found another way to suggest I could change her flat and she could be on her way promptly. She went beyond informing me this time and assured me it was the transmission, that she had called a wrecker, and that she couldn't wait to get home to tell her husband that the transmission about which she had been complaining had finally blown. They would fix her transmission, and he would pay the bill. She was going to hold him accountable.

Did I mention that leaders need to get their facts straight before they start holding others accountable? With her gratitude for stopping, I went along to LAX and returned home.

It was an instructive experience for me. Because the woman had a focus that was different from mine, my well-intentioned exercise was wasted. There is other exercise that is important for leaders.

Discussion Questions

1. Whom do you know that is a master of positive accountability? Is it worth the leader's time to do this faithfully? What outcome have you seen?

2. Have you seen a situation where positive and negative accountability weren't balanced? How did it affect the organization's culture, and what impact, if any, did it have on individuals?

3. Do you know of a time when a leader held others accountable with more diligence than he held himself accountable? What was the result?

4. How is showing accountability related to another principle in this book?

5. When a leader has to do a superior's bidding in firing a subordinate for cause or to accommodate a budget, what are things the leader needs to remember to do and

not to do? Do any other principles we have covered apply?

6. Do you know of a case when a leader, other than Daniel, didn't denigrate those who were making it tough if not unfair for him? What was the outcome?

7. How can a leader balance positive and negative accountability? How can a leader balance both parts of accountability: showing it in him- or herself and requiring it of others? In which of these areas are your strengths and weaknesses?

8. Have you or someone you know ever been premature in assigning fault? What was the situation, and how did you or that person handle it? What did you learn?

Ten
EXERCISE REGULARLY

"ARE YOU SURE PULLUPS ARE PART OF THE MALE TEST?"

Leadership with regard to oneself is to exercise regularly. Exercise comes in more forms than the physical, but that is a good place to start.

Physical Exercise

The virtues of physical exercise are well documented. Along with a proper diet, regular exercise can contribute to good health and longevity.

I have observed that good physical exercise makes one more alert and productive on the job. On days when I work out in the early morning before going to work, I almost get a rush midway through the morning. This defies reason for those of us without medical training, because it seems on the surface that if you use up energy early, it won't be available later. In fact, it's just the opposite. Exercising early provides a sustained burst of energy that brings along alertness and productivity. That has been my experience.

I have also found that I can work at a higher level and for a longer time if I'm exercising regularly. Fitness experts can say how much, at what rate, and for how long one should exercise, but for me it has very positive benefits. I haven't had the mid-afternoon slumps when exercise is part of my routine. To be candid, I haven't always taken the time to exercise as I should, so I'm speaking from experience on this mid-afternoon slump business. Perhaps you know what I mean.

There is a wealth of material about other medical issues that exercise can fight off: obesity, diabetes, heart disease, and respiratory issues. Suffice it to say, physical exercise is of enormous benefit to leaders and followers alike. But leaders who exercise only their bodies are ignoring other ways to promote effectiveness on a personal level. Consider that healthy minds live in healthy bodies.

Mental Exercise

Mental exercise is just as important as physical exercise, though it seldom receives as much attention. But just as physical exercise stimulates and strengthens the body, so mental exercise does the mind. And a leader needs a mind that is both stimulated and strong.

The benefits of mental exercise closely parallel those of physical exercise. Mental nimbleness helps leaders move from the grand strategic level to the detailed tactical level and then back again with ease, allowing a leader to "wrap his mind" around knotty, paradoxical, and complex issues.

A leader needs mental endurance to work at high-performance levels in meeting after meeting the same in the late afternoon as in the early morning. A mentally strong leader can work out of his or her comfort zone when necessary. For me this has been jet engine and metallurgy engineering issues, programmatic financial issues, and fifth and sixth generation consequences to what-if drills.

Here are some ways to exercise to build up mental flexibility, endurance, and strength.

The first exercise is reading. As I discussed in Chapter 7, good leaders are good readers.

A second exercise is listening. Leaders learn much by listening. Too often, leaders interrupt the telling of a problem and deprive themselves of important details. There may be a point when the leader needs to bring the discussion back to a topic or give others an opportunity to talk, so there is a delicate balance here. But it is useful to listen a little more than one naturally wants to.

Listening has benefits beyond gathering information. Sometimes people can talk themselves through a problem and right into the solution. When they do this on their own, or when the skilled leader-listener guides them in that direction, the solution becomes the "child" of the talker. The person's ownership of the problem will be stronger than if the leader had directed it.

Still another benefit of listening is that onlookers see the leader's genuine interest and willingness to learn from others, which may motivate or inspire the witnesses to do the same.

A third exercise I call engaging, that is, participating in conversations and discussions on topics about which we aren't authoritative. This can push our recall and ability to organize our thoughts. It puts our listening ability to the test while drawing from the reservoir of what we have read and heard before.

Like in relationships, it steps up our game from getting acquainted with an idea to wrestling with its implications in preparation for embracing it as our own. Engaging in dialogue and debates, formal and informal, is mental exercise.

A fourth is sport. I use this word to keep the parallel with the physical going. Like on the physical side, there are things leaders can do that are just pure exercise with some side benefits like satisfaction, camaraderie, and increased alertness.

Mental games come in individual and group forms. Individual games include crossword puzzles (not my favorite) and Sudoku (my preference). Group games include various card games, board games, and interaction games. The list of these is nearly endless. Some are more fun than exercise, but competitive leaders will find a way to get exercise when others are just having fun.

A fifth is writing. As I am finding out by putting my thoughts into readable words here, writing focuses the mind and provides opportunity to clarify ambiguities. Writing is as much a mental exercise as speaking, reading, listening, and the others.

It is no accident that I have devoted twice as much space to mental exercise as I did to physical exercise. The former gets a lot of attention, the latter less. The wise leader will keep both in balance, along with a third, spiritual exercise.

Spiritual Exercise

If physical exercise is discussed the most and mental exercise less, I would suggest that spiritual exercise is almost never discussed outside institutions where it is better understood and embraced. In some places, leaders have to be careful about discussing this matter publicly for reasons of undue command influence. Fortunately, our nation isn't to the place where the exercise is prohibited, but we are less free to discuss it than in the past.

The spiritual part of us is just as real as the physical and mental parts. Blaise Pascal wrote in *Pensées*, "There is a God shaped vacuum in the heart of every man which cannot be filled by any created thing, but only by God, the Creator, made known through Jesus." The author of the New Testament book of Hebrews wrote "But without faith it is impossible to please [God]" (11:6).

So how do we exercise spiritually? Is it enough to go to church on Sunday and to pray before meals? Would it be enough on the physical side to go to a basketball game once a week and read box scores at the dinner table?

For decades, I have started my days reading Scripture methodically and thoughtfully and praying for those in need, including myself. I have prayed for my chain of command, and when I told a president that I prayed for him, he expressed great appreciation. I have seen scores of prayers answered by the One who shows us "great and mighty things which thou knowest not" (Jeremiah 33:3).

I have found that memorized Scripture provides comfort and guidance when I need it, and it stills my racing mind when I need sleep. Meditating isn't just for mystics. David wrote in Psalm 1 that the blessed man has "his delight in the law of the LORD; and in his law doth he meditate day and night" (1:2).

Singing and listening to good music exercises the spiritual part of us too. Unlike any other creature, humans have the ability to match words and music at the same time. We can also hear a tune and know the words that attach to it even if it's a tune from years in the past. Sometimes words to old hymns I sang as a schoolboy come to mind with something someone will say or a snatch of another tune I hear. It takes me back to the text and context of that grand old hymn. One example is John Newton's (1725-1807) "Amazing Grace."

The Lord has promised good to me.
His word my hope secures.
He will my shield and portion be,
As long as life endures.

I also find some classical music very compatible with spiritual exercise, particularly the works of Bach, Beethoven, and Brahms.

Hymns are spiritual and can be edifying. The lyrics can be worthy of meditation as they point one's heart to the Savior. And classical music provides a soul setting that often inspires meditation on God's Word, His attributes, and His love for us.

As with mental exercise, listening is good spiritual exercise. There are dozens of excellent speakers who have devoted their lives to challenging the spiritual part of us. Some of them are in our local churches, and you can hear others on the radio, CDs, the Internet, and television.

Similarly, some authors have devoted their writings to challenging and growing the spiritual part of us. Taking time to delve into this kind of reading is good spiritual exercise.

Finally, as on the physical side, gathering with like-minded folks contributes to spiritual exercise. While there is value to being alone with one's Maker, there is also value in "assembling…together" (Hebrews 10:25) with others for corporate worship, teaching, and fellowship.

There is another delicate matter that bears discussion here. In some non-Christian circles, there is a reluctance to discuss spiritual things openly. I mentioned the importance to avoid undue command influence.

It is also true, however, given the spiritual part of us and the need to balance it with the physical and mental parts, leaders do well to acknowledge the spiritual side of every individual, including themselves.

It is as important for a leader to exercise spiritually as it is for him to provide a comfort zone for subordinates to do the same. I have seen young men and women praying before going into combat and again after returning from the mission, and there was neither a chaplain present nor any command influence. They just felt the need and did it. Leaders need to provide for the freedom to exercise without necessarily calling out the cadence of the calisthenics.

Unlike physical and mental exercises that are inherently helpful, some kinds of spiritual exercise also require application. Reading God's Word, for example, is helpful, but applying what you read is necessary. The Apostle James wrote, "But be ye doers of the Word, and not hearers only, deceiving your own selves" (James 1:22).

The Priority

A fair question to ask at this point is: Which of the three—physical, mental, and spiritual—has the highest priority? You will get different answers depending where you look.

If you look in mass media, physical wins by a landslide. Myriad are the advertisements for beauty products, food, drink, clothing, and all things temporal.

If you look in Scripture, you'll find a different emphasis. In the Sermon on the Mount, Jesus said:

> Take no thought for your life, what ye shall eat, or what ye shall drink; nor yet for your body what ye shall put on. Is not the life more than meat, and the body than raiment? (Matthew 6:25)

Jesus taught us what is most important.

> But seek ye first the kingdom of God, and His right-
> eousness; and all these things shall be added unto you.
> (Matthew 6:33)

The Teacher who created the physical and lived in it, and Who came from and then returned to the spiritual, put the latter first. So should we.

Physical Profit

This is not to say there is no value in the physical. Physical exercise does have value, as I laid out earlier. The Apostle Paul agreed with this, as he wrote to Timothy, his protégé:

> For bodily exercise profiteth little: but godliness is prof-
> itable unto all things, having promise of the life that
> now is, and of that which is to come. (1 Timothy 4:8)

The point that Paul is making is that bodily exercise profits during this lifetime. So it *is* profitable. But godliness is profitable in the life to come, that is, eternity. So we have the physical profitable for our lifetime and the spiritual for eternity. Physical exercise is good, but spiritual exercise is better.

The Parchments

There is an obscure verse at the end of the last letter that the Apostle Paul wrote. Paul asks Timothy to come to him quickly. We find a strange request sandwiched in between two lists of names of people involved in the ministry. Paul writes:

> The cloak that I left at Troas with Carpus, when thou
> comest, bring with thee, and the books, but especially
> the parchments. (2 Timothy 4:13)

Paul asked for the cloak, an outer garment. He had a specific one in mind—"the" cloak. He wanted it for warmth—clearly the physical. Though this reference to the physical isn't about strength or exercise, two other verses clearly are:

> I therefore so run, not as uncertainly; so fight I, not as one that beateth the air. But I keep under my body, and bring it into subjection. (1 Corinthians 9:26, 27a)

> The glory of young men is their strength: and the beauty of old men is the gray head. (Proverbs 20:29)

He asked for the books. Then as now, books are for the mind; they are for mental exercise. Paul apparently knew he was at the end of his life, but he still wanted to exercise mentally.

He also asked for the parchments. These parchments were the documents that professional scribes had painstakingly produced. They had copied the Scriptures over those early centuries before and after the time of Christ. Paul asked not only for some physical and mental things, but also for that which would exercise him spiritually.

But note the word *especially*. He wanted all three, but he especially wanted the parchments, the Word of God. He wanted physical exercise and mental exercise, yes, but especially spiritual exercise.

He was saying, "Timothy, if you have to leave some of them behind, I want you to bring the parchments without fail." Here in a single verse we see all three, "but especially the parchments."

Mandatory Fitness

During my days in the Air Force, we always had some form of fitness testing and usually a fitness program to accompany it. They aren't synonymous. A program without testing has no evaluation to standards. Testing without a program seldom produces the desired test outcomes.

In my early days, I remember running the required mile and a half easily. My breathing was the limiting factor in those days. As the years and decades passed, strength and pain joined in.

When push-ups and sit-ups were added, that brought along new dimensions—all good. Finally, waist circumference was added because of the positive correlation the medical community determined it had to cardiac health (as I recall).

With all this, I still found the test targets reasonable so long as I exercised throughout the year. If we tested at or above 90% of the goals, we didn't have to test again until a year later. If we scored above passing but below 90%, we would have to take the test each six months.

Obviously, the goal was fitness, not high scores. The former facilitated the latter, not vice versa!

Mental Food

In my last position in the Air Force before retiring, I worked at the Pentagon and was responsible for the policy that governed, among other things, logistics and aircraft maintenance matters. To be clear, there were many involved in this methodical and incremental process, but the buck stopped at my desk.

I found it very useful to regularly visit the people working in aircraft maintenance and logistics so I could assess current policy and the need for change. This kept the procedures and practices both current and safe.

Usually on these visits I would tour the flight line and maintenance back-shops, meet with the squadron and group leaders, and talk with young airmen doing the work of maintainers and logisticians. At lunch I would meet with officers and share with them whatever was on my mind about policy changes, areas of emphasis from headquarters, leadership thoughts, and career development updates. I always emphasized safety and compliance with technical data—the bedrock foundation of safe and efficient logistics.

On a visit to McGuire Air Force Base in New Jersey, I decided to listen at lunch rather than talk. I asked each of the thirty or so officers to stand and tell me their name, what they did, why they came into the Air Force, what they liked best about it, and what they liked least about it. I got an earfull!

At the start, the first one or two were careful about the negatives, but things got rolling along quickly. I needed to hear what was on their minds. I wanted the unvarnished thoughts of these young folks who would be carrying out the policies we wrote at the headquarters. I needed to know what was working well and what wasn't. It was mental exercise for me—necessary and helpful on several levels.

Fifth-Grade Perspective

When I was a captain between 1978 and 1981, I was active in a local Baptist church and taught a Sunday school class of fourth, fifth, and sixth graders.

One Sunday, I was teaching a lesson, the main point of which was that we should read God's Word regularly. At the end of the lesson, I circled back around to see if they had caught my main point.

I asked it plainly, "How often should we read the Bible?" A young fellow named Ronnie offered, "Once a year." Underwhelmed, I chatted with him in the hearing of the entire class about needing to do it more often than just once a year. He amended, "How about once every month?" I had the same chat, and thankfully, he amended again to, "Is it once a week?"

Pleased with the progress of his answers in the right direction, though not to the response of "daily" that I sought, I suggested to the entire class we should read our Bibles every day. To that, Ronnie said aloud with some frustration, "But Mr. Reno, it's a long Bible." I had meant to read *from* the Bible, but he had taken me literally.

The point is that spiritual exercise on a regular basis strengthens a leader for his or her demanding duties.

We have seen the virtues of setting the course and pace, showing accountability, and exercising regularly. These three actions form my leadership model.

Discussion Questions

1. What are the benefits and liabilities of regular physical exercise?

2. What are the benefits and risks of mental exercise?

3. To what extent does physical, mental, or spiritual exercise impact either of the other two?

4. Have you known anyone who properly drew the line between spiritual exercise without infringing on the rights of others? How did he or she do this? Do you see this as being more or less difficult in the coming years?

5. Have you or anyone you know properly balanced exercise in these three domains? What did that look like?

6. What time of day have you found to be the best time to tend to the "parchments"? What are the problems for you in planning to do it at other times? Should there be a single time each day? Why or why not?

7. Emotional exercise is noticeably absent from this list of three. Is it of equal or greater weight to any of the three? What would emotional exercise look like?

ELEVEN

A LEADERSHIP MODEL

In the preceding three chapters, I have shared three leadership maneuvers that have served me well over more than a few years. I have used them when in command and when in staff positions. I have modified them over the years. For example, I used to advocate "require accountability," but now I say "show accountability" for reasons I discussed in chapter nine. I have carved them into what I call "a leadership model."

A Model

I have found that having a leadership model helps me think about the right things often and at the right times.

A leadership model synopsizes some of the important elements of leadership into something that is practical and useful. It is not a list of the definitions of leadership, though that would be helpful. It is not a bibliography of books and articles on leadership, which would exceed the scope of this book.

It is not a compendium of leadership traits about which so many have written. It is not a chronology of leadership practitioners, famous and notorious, and what they have practiced, though that would afford intrigue at least in some cases.

It is none of these, and it certainly is not all of these.

Indeed, we like to read leadership books and hear inspiring speakers talk about leadership. But how do we move from the experiences of others to improving our lead?

A leadership model helps one think about the right things at the right time. It helps a leader talk about expectations to subordinates in a coordinated and consistent way. It helps leaders remember in the heat of battle what they intended when they were out of the fray.

My Model

I have taken the content of chapters 8 through 10 and formed it into a leadership model that has worked for me. Let me summarize.

I put the mission first because, at the end of the day, a leader's superior or shareholders will be looking for mission accomplishment. In a business, it's the bottom line. In the military, it's the mission. In education, it's academics. In a library, it's information. In sales, it's revenue. You get the drift.

It is imperative to know exactly what the mission is and how various stakeholders view it. This is an important job for the leader. It is also critical for a leader to communicate the mission consistently, clearly, and repeatedly so that the followers "get it."

As retired General Roger Brady notes in his book *Forget Success,* not everyone agrees on which is more important: people or mission. He cites the amazing success of Southwest Airlines under Herb Kelleher's inspiring leadership and his focus on people. I don't argue with my friend, General Brady. As he affirms, success needs both.

I do not understate the importance of people in the art of leadership because it is all about people. A leader who doesn't pay attention to the people won't be successful over the long haul, and maybe not even over the short haul. Every once in a while, a leader needs to look over his shoulder to be sure someone is following. Let me be clear: the people are critical.

So I put the mission first with the people right after. Last, comes myself. When I was in the Air Force, our second core value was "service before self." The word *service* didn't mean the branch of the armed forces called the Air Force as much as it did the act of serving. Serving the mission and others has to come before oneself. Mission and others aren't exclusive to self, only ahead of it.

Thus my leadership model puts leadership with regard to the mission first, leadership with regard to others second, and leadership with regard to myself third. What you read in chapters eight, nine, and ten then matches up with these:

- Mission: set the course and pace
- Others: show accountability
- Self: exercise regularly

That is my leadership model, but it probably isn't or shouldn't be yours. It worked for me because it was the way I am wired. It was specific to my experience, it suited my responsibilities, and it matched my values and priorities. It is not intended to be everything there is to know about leadership, but rather it is a concise set of three things to do that helped me along the leadership path.

Your Model

I have explored the elements of my leadership model at some length, I have briefly looked at what a model is, and I tied together the bow of these two. Now let's move along to your leadership model.

For the reasons stated earlier, it is important to craft a model that is tailored to you. After I had been teaching this for several years, my wife asked me how to do what I was suggesting people do. I thought doing these things was just intuitive. But it isn't for everyone. So here are some questions to guide you in forming your model:

1. Think through and then list your *priorities,* your *influence spheres,* and *your principal roles.*

   FIRST, list the priorities. I have a fondness for Micah 6:8, which says to "do justly, and love mercy, and to walk humbly with thy God." Those are good priorities. I have a distinguished friend whom I deeply respect who would list four F's here: Faith, Family, Firm, and Friends. Some others would use the JOY acronym: Jesus, others, and you. This is an important starting point in developing your leadership model: What are your priorities?

   SECOND, list your spheres of influence. You should consider those places where you live and operate and where you have influence on others. If you're a pastor, it's your church. If a coach, it's your team. Perhaps it's as a husband or wife, as a mother or father, as a teacher or administrator. What are your influence spheres?

   THIRD, list your principal roles. By this I mean the actions you do that rise to the top in frequency or importance. A partial list would include the following: to oversee, account, provide, pray, preach, teach, encourage, and show. There are many more. What are your principal roles?

2. What are your most valued leadership actions? There are many from which to choose, but you should pick the ones you value the most. Examples are: direct, serve, encourage, inspire, communicate, and recognize; show integrity, excellence, tenacity, and competence; and be organized, visible, transparent, humble, and open. This list isn't in any particular order, nor is the list exhaustive, only illustrative. What are your most valued leadership actions?

3. What *actions* best cover your priorities, spheres, and roles? In other words, which of what you listed in #2 cover what you listed in #1?

4. Reduce the number to *three*. You may have come up with five or more actions in #3, and that is fine. Now, through combining and refining, reduce the list to just three. I have found that lists that are longer than three actions or maneuvers defy memory. You may need to go back and review the first two steps, but try hard to reduce the number of actions to just three.

5. Put them in the *right order*. In my model, I explained the rationale of the order. You don't have to agree with that, but you should put your model in order. This is a good time to align it with your priorities, spheres, and roles. This step should take considerable thought and might be worthy of revisiting over time.

6. Add *creativity* to ease recall. It will help your recall and serve as a mnemonic device for others if you can find a creative way to array your actions. Note I used the template of "mission, others, and self." I have seen some

use alliteration and others an abbreviation, the name of a place, the initials of a friend, or an acronym. One computer science student began each of his three words with "a, s, and d"—the first three letters on the left hand at a computer keyboard. Pick something that works for you; personalize it.

7. Show the *biblical basis*. You have noticed in the three elements of my model that I used verses, stories, and characters from the Bible. I want leadership maneuvers that are strong enough to be backed with Scripture. One can do no better. If your model goes against Scripture, use it at your own peril. If your familiarity with Scripture falls short of being able to do this, ask someone who could help you. That person is probably willing. You and your model will be better for it.

8. Include a *personal story* for each action. I have found that my stories are longer and more fondly remembered than the points I want to make, so I try to use the stories as transporters. Cultural sensitivity is important, and so is a balance between successes and failures. A little self-deprecation goes a long way. The best leader storytellers pick on themselves, not others.

This model is a how-to that I hope is useful for you. You'll find a sample model development worksheet in Appendix B and a list of models some others have developed in sessions where I have taught this recently in Appendix C. This latter list may give you some ideas, but be sure to tailor your model to your situation, not theirs.

Discussion Questions

1. What spheres of influence did you design your model to cover?

2. What is your leadership model?

3. Why did you put the elements of your model in the order you chose?

4. What questions does your model remind you to ask?

5. What personal anecdote for one of the points of your model will most inspire others?

6. You'll need to adjust your model if something in your life changes significantly. What do you expect that to be and when will it occur?

CONCLUSION

I do not intend this book to be a definitive source on leadership. Rather, it is a compilation of the musings and experiences of a leader on whom the Lord has had His hand. Those musings and experiences have centered on ten leadership maneuvers I have seen work for formal and informal leaders, and for leaders of small and large organizations alike.

Themes of this book include the following:

- Leaders have integrity in action, speech, and thought.
- Service is the foundation of leadership.
- Humility is essential in a leader's role as a follower, leader, and child of God.

If I only had the time on an elevator ride to tell you what this book was about, my "elevator speech" would sound like this: Leaders are servants—they serve before and after they are elevated. They look for opportunities to serve, they give credit and take blame, they ask for help, they read, they set the course and pace, they hold themselves and others accountable, and they exercise regularly. They feed their leadership with the meat of serving.

It is foundational to good leadership to call things what they truly are. The anecdotes in the preceding chapters bear this out. Whether it is taking blame, sharing credit, or showing and expecting accountability, part of showing justice is responding appropriately and consistently. It is complex and difficult to perfectly balance justice, mercy, and humility, but good leaders work at it all the time. This biblical exhortation is both timeless and doable.

Leadership is a journey. My navigator stories not only illustrate the book's maneuvers, they also provide a metaphor for leadership. We need good compasses to help us find our way. Everyone needs help along the way, especially leaders. The leadership journey is marked by ups and downs, by headwinds and tailwinds, by calm and rough air, and by stormy and clear skies. I haven't always gotten things right, as you have read, and I don't always know what tomorrow holds, but I know Who holds tomorrow.

Appendix A
What the Humble Do

This is a "parking lot" for some thoughts on what humility looks like in flesh and blood, or, said another way, what the humble do.

We have touched on humility in three chapters of this book: Chapter 1, "The Greatest is a Servant," Chapter 2, "Show Justice, Mercy, and Humility," and Chapter 3, "Seek to Serve." The theme of humility runs throughout this book, from the Introduction to chapter ten, with putting the mission and others before oneself. This fleshes out those thoughts in more detail along with Scriptural references and some story snippets.

Earlier, we said that, according to the Free Dictionary website, "humility is a form of the word *humble*, which means, 'marked by meekness or modesty of behavior, attitude, or spirit; not arrogant or prideful; showing deferential or submissive respect.'" Note that while humility is an attitude, it is also a behavior, and it is marked by meekness and modesty, or understating. Deference and submission are synonyms of humility; arrogance and pride are antonyms.

In April 2013, the chapter of the Delta Mu Delta national honor society for business majors at Cedarville University asked me to speak on this topic at their annual recognition banquet. That undergraduate students at the top of their academic game would be so interested in "humility" overwhelmed me. It revealed to me some things about their high character. I hope you find my notes from that night useful.

1. Seek God's not man's praise.
   - Colossians 3:23: "Whatever you do...do it...as to the Lord."
   - Defer gratification.

2. Look to the needs of others.
   - Philippians 2:4: "Look not every man on his own things, but...also on the things of others."
   - Proverbs 11:27: "He that diligently seeketh good procureth favor."
   - James 1:27: Pure religion: Visit the fatherless and widows.
   - The Good Samaritan story answers the question, "Who is my neighbor?" but also illustrates helping the needy.

3. Others can elevate you higher than you can.
   - James 4:10: "Humble yourselves in the sight of the Lord, and he shall lift you up."
   - Genesis 41:4: "See, I have set thee over all the land of Egypt."
   - Luke 14:8-9: Moving up in seating.
   - I knew a general mistakenly seated on the second row at a ceremony. He sat quietly. When the mistake was discovered, he was asked to move up to the front row and to the place of honor he deserved.

4. Learn from disappointments.
   - Genesis 37, 39: Joseph, 20 pieces of silver to overseer.
   - Job 1-2, 42: Job blessed "double."
   - When my career path changed from aircrew operations to maintenance and logistics, I was disheartened but learned quickly it had a far better upside for me.

5. See things from an eternal perspective.
   - Matthew 6: Alms, prayer, fasting, treasure in heaven.

6. Be quicker to admit fault than to assign it.
   - Nehemiah 1:6-7: "Both I and my father's house have sinned, we have dealt very corruptly."

- University student e-mail to professor: "Honestly it was my error. I should have thought to ask but did not. I should be held to the same punishment that you are accustomed to giving for a late paper."

7. Let another praise you and not yourself.
   - Proverbs 27:2: "Let another man praise thee, and not thine own mouth, a stranger and not thine own lips."
   - Human nature wants to blow one's own horn; others can play a sweeter melody.

8. Serve your way to the top.
   - Matthew 20:27: "Whosever will be chief among you, let him be your servant."
   - Sound leadership principle: Knowing the needs of your peers, people.
   - *Undercover Boss* television series, where the boss went undercover to the roots of organization to see what was really going on, should be common practice.
   - "Servant-in-Chief" would be a wonderful duty title… for all.

9. Respect others.
   - John 4:9-10: Woman of Samaria, "no dealings."
   - John 8:48: Jews to Jesus, "… thou art a Samaritan." No response.
   - Jonathan-David, then David-Jonathan-Mephibosheth.

10. Show others respect.
    - Philemon v8-9: Paul beseeched instead of enjoining (command, impose).
    - 1 Timothy 2:1-2: (Pray) for kings and for all that are in authority.
    - My boss asked me for a member of my staff and made an appointment with me in my office to ask. He had access to all I had and didn't have to ask…but did.

APPENDIX B

LEADERSHIP MODEL WORKSHEET

1. Think through and then list:
    a. Your priorities:
    b. Your spheres of influence:
    c. Your principal role(s):
2. List the leadership actions you value most highly:
3. What leadership actions best cover your priorities, spheres of influence, and roles?
4. If possible, reduce the number of actions to 3:
    1.
    2.
    3.
5. Put the actions in the "right" order:
    1.
    2.
    3.
6. Add creativity to ease remembering:
    1.
    2.
    3.
7. What is the biblical basis for each action?
    Action: *Biblical Basis:*
    1.
    2.
    3.
8. What memorable, personal story illustrates each action done well or not well?
    Action: *Illustration gist:*
    1.
    2.
    3.

Appendix C

Other Leadership Models

This listing of leadership models comes from the work of administrators, commanders, leaders of small and large organizations and institutions, more than a few college students, and men of history. As mentioned in Chapter 11, each has the originality and applicability of the leader who designed them.

There would be much that goes with each example to explain it in the way of personal background, personal biblical application, and personal experience. Yours would and should be different. These are intended to be illustrative for you, yet neither descriptive nor entirely applicable.

1. 3-C's: Character, Competence, Commitment
2. 3-C's: Character, Competence, Communication
3. 3-C's: Character, Communication, Caring (General Roger Brady, USAF, Ret.)
4. 3-S's: Swift to hear, Slow to speak, Slow to wrath (James 1:9)
5. 3-C's: Character, Competence, Capacity (2 Timothy 3:17, Lee C. Reno)
6. 3-E's: Example, Encourage, Exercise
7. 4-L's: Listen, Love, Laugh, Lead by example
8. 3-S's: Stewardship, Shepherd, Sacrifice
9. 3-S's: Service, Structure, Set an example
10. CASS: controlled Competence, applied Accountability, sacrificial Serving, Steady Self-discipline (Cass[ie] Gray)
11. CEO: Confidence, Example, Organization
12. OLE: Organize, Lead, Encourage

13. SEA: Service and sacrifice, Embracing everyone, Authenticity and attitude
14. VIP: Vision, Influence, Passion
15. Exemplify servant-hood of Christ, Listen to others, be Informed
16. Faithful, Compassion, Confidentiality
17. Follow faithfully, Serve humbly, Live passionately
18. Lead by Example, through Service, with Courage
19. Leading with Integrity, with Commitment, through international Service for others
20. Listen and learn, Live and give, Competent and caring
21. Many watch for one, Audience of one, One for many
22. Obey God, Set an example, Invest in others
23. Strength, Loyalty, Justice
24. Self-reverence, Self-knowledge, Self-control (Sir Alford Lord Tennyson)
25. Practice self-denial and self-control, as well as the strictest economy in all financial matters (General Robert E. Lee)
25. Team, Integrity, Excellence

About the Author

Loren Reno, Lt. Gen. USAF (Ret), earned a BA in comprehensive science and education from Cedarville University, Ohio; an MS in systems management from University of Southern California; completed his military and national security studies at Air University; and graduate studies at Harvard University, Syracuse University, and University of North Carolina. Loren has always loved teaching and coaching, and his path took him to both at the highest levels, before he worked his way up through the ranks in the military. During his thirty-eight years in the US Air Force, he was a five-time commander in maintenance and logistics, served in combat, and led organizations small and large, before retiring in the grade of Lieutenant General. Loren's wife and three children followed him as he moved from the flight lines at air bases to the corridors of the Pentagon, from positions in aircraft operations and maintenance to logistics and leadership. Presently the dean of the school of business administration at his alma mater, Cedarville University, Loren enjoys music, reading, and traveling, and he still teaches and coaches.

Contact Loren:
loren.reno68@gmail.com